PARTNERING WITH JES
TWELVE PEOPLE IN YOUR LIFE

just 12.

JAKE KIRCHNER
SCOTT KNOLLENBERG

 good soil press

Just 12 © Jake Kirchner and Scott Knollenberg. Except as provided by the Copyright Act (1978) no part of this publication may be reproduced, stored in a retrieval system, or transmitted in any form or by any means without the prior written permission of the publisher.

ISBN: 978-1-7370394-3-3

Library of Congress Control Number: 2021910927

Print book first edition

Printed in the United States of America

First Printing 2021

Cover and Interior Design: The Brand Office

All Scripture quotations, unless otherwise indicated, are taken from the Holy Bible, New International Version®, NIV®. Copyright ©1973, 1978, 1984, 2011 by Biblica, Inc.™ Used by permission of Zondervan. All rights reserved worldwide. www.zondervan.com The "NIV" and "New International Version" are trademarks registered in the United States Patent and Trademark Office by Biblica, Inc.™

Acknowledgments

Pete and Laurie Zeman, owners of Lorrayne Ranch in Guffey, Colorado, who insisted we write this book.

All our early adaptors from Church at HighPoint, Institute for Community, and Community Life in Romeoville, Illinois, who have started their journey to 12.

Scott's leadership cohorts, Tom, Sean, Alicia, and Hannah, who helped start this Just 12 journey with us 2 years ago.

Clifton Ross, a friend and pastor, who coined the term "Just 12" after hearing the vision.

Christi Neill, who was the first of many who provided valuable feedback on the content of this book.

Cathy Wood, who encouraged Jake to let things simmer on the back burner and wait for the right time to start cooking.

Dean Danielson, who keeps cheering Jake on to be bold.

Our wives...who have been quick to sacrifice and quick to listen. And who have said "keep going" more times than we can count.

Table of Contents

Introduction

"The whole point of collaboration
is that you give and take from
each other, and that's how you
create things that are
totally new."

– *Virgil Abloh*

It has been about a year since Scott asked me to write this book with him. You will notice that it's actually me, Jake, doing the writing. There are a few reasons for this. One, I like to write a lot more than Scott. Two, as we talked about the flow and tone of the book, we agreed it would be easier to follow just one voice/storyteller versus going back and forth and trying to differentiate and remember who was saying what. Three, Scott didn't really want to write a book. It was never his intention. It took the enthusiasm and encouragement of Pete and Laurie Zeman, Scott's friends and fellow dreamers, to even put the idea in his head. A few weeks later, on a late night in the fall of 2019 at Miller's Ale House, Scott and I got to talking, and we have talked nearly every week since. The countless video conversations, texts, and occasional face-to-face meals were the groundwork for each chapter. Each week we would brainstorm, work on content and flow and revise and refine. Although it is my fingers tapping on the keyboard, each idea has the impression of Scott imprinted into it.

Handing Over the Keys

I heard about Scott before I ever met him. I was visiting a friend's church, where Scott was an attender. The church was finishing up a capital campaign for a building project. My friend shared with me all the plans for a building that would host events and organizations that would help develop artists and performers from the community. As we walked the grounds of the future site, he shared the story of a guy who sold his dream car and gave the proceeds to the project. That guy was Scott. What I later learned about Scott, and have observed ever since, is that he continues to give his life to Jesus and the things Jesus is up to. All those years ago he was convinced that Jesus was up to something in that community. He is still planted firmly in that place, even though that church is no longer present there. Jesus once told His followers that He would hand them the keys to the kingdom.[1] Scott made that idea his own and handed his keys over for the sake of the kingdom.

The building that Scott gave his dream car to help build is the place where he and I shared countless dreams and visions about helping others follow Jesus in ways that would transform our world. For a few years, he was my boss; but even in those years, he was my friend—perhaps more like an older brother (a much older brother, I like to think). Scott and I have been on a long journey that has culminated in the content of these pages. The journey continues as we seek to live out what we are imploring others to start doing.

We have learned a lot from each other, and have shared what we have learned from others. Sometimes it is difficult to remember where an idea originated—if it was him or me or some author that we read. In reality, any idea that is worth pursuing in our desire to follow Jesus was initiated by God's Spirit. Still, we must acknowledge some people as pivotal to our thinking, and subsequently, this book. Our time together at an innovative and fast-growing multi-site church outside of Chicago is where our journey started and is foundational by default. We are grateful for the culture that helped shape us and that, for a brief time, we were able to help shape. In that time, we were introduced to Alan Hirsh, Kim Hammond, and Mike Frost.[2] Once we started down a path with these missional thinkers, we discovered Mike Breen, Neil Cole, David Fitch, and Hugh Halter. If you are familiar with any of them, you will recognize their voices echoing in the margins. If you are unfamiliar with them, we encourage you to interact with something they have created.

You will notice footnotes in many places that refer to Scripture. The complete verse referenced can be found in the back of the book. We understand that some readers are not as familiar with finding and reading Scripture, so we hope this helps.

For the sake of context, Scott is married and has a high school-age daughter. Scott was once on the business fast track to becoming an executive at a Fortune 100 company. When I met him, he had left that path to become a children's pastor at the aforementioned church...I told you he will give his life for Jesus and what Jesus is up to. He eventually became a campus pastor. He is currently working in community development and volunteering as a pastor. I'm married as well and have three kids, boy-girl-boy, six, seven and nine. When I first met Scott, I was volunteering in the student ministry where I would eventually become the Student Director. I was part of helping several other campuses and churches launch before moving to Minnesota, where I currently reside. I served as an outreach and connections pastor for three years before transitioning to my current role as a stay-at-home parent. A good chunk of the time writing this book has been spent in what feels like an alternate reality dominated by the virus called COVID-19.

Just 12 has come to us more as sets of striking realizations than as a subject we set out to research and study. Research and study has come, through many trials and errors, mistakes and missteps, as well as results worth celebrating. This is the place we have arrived, and yet we do not feel as if everything is settled. We are not about to hunker down, as if there is nowhere else to go or as if this is the end of discovery. There is still much to learn. What is proposed in the chapters ahead is still being tested in our lives.

We trust that as more people give *Just 12* a diligent try, much will be revealed in its effectiveness and flaws. What we share has, and is, dramatically reshaping how we relate to everyone in our lives every day. Our goal is that everyday, ordinary, Jesus-oriented people would begin the same journey. Our prayer is that it will do in your life what it is doing in ours, which is giving us new insight into just how openhanded God is in partnering with us in forming our world through reforming our relationships in it. This new framework is inspiring and motivating us toward a previously unmatched intentionality with the people God has placed in our paths. And it is simplifying how we engage and experience the community of faith, the church. May it do all those things, and more, for you.

What Jesus Could Have Done

"If you had one shot
or one opportunity
to seize everything you ever
wanted in one moment,
would you capture it..."

–EMINEM, *LOSE YOURSELF*

CHAPTER 1

50 HOURS

Steve and I stood ten feet away from a two-foot-high pile of ice cubes awaiting an explosion. It was a cool late-September night, and like most nights, we were just looking for something fun to do. There is nothing more suspicious than two fourteen-year-old boys loitering about in the back alley of Bon Gusto's Italian Restaurant and the Handy Andy's Hardware Store. The discarded ice, slowly melting in the grass a few feet from the back door of the small restaurant, was an ideal location for our experiment. Inches below the ice was a plastic pop bottle, slowly expanding from the chemical reaction caused by its contents. The concoction brewing below the ice was affectionately known in our neighborhood as a "Works Bomb." It had little ability to do what its name implied, except in creating a very loud—and oftentimes startling—boom. We were determined to test exactly what the capacities of such a distributive device might be. My older brother, Gabe, (who, by the way, was the one who taught us how to make the now infamous "Works Bomb") spotted us as he made his way to the

7-Eleven convenience store to grab a blue-raspberry slushie and use the pay phone. Intrigued by our brilliant idea, he stood a few feet away on the opposite side of our test site. The timeline for this kind of thing was unpredictable, so Gabe left. And just in time.

Headlights suddenly reflected off the glistening chunks of melting ice. Only one car ever parked in that spot: a 1994 electric blue Ford Mustang Convertible. It had black racing stripes and a black canvas top. It also held a person behind the wheel that had little love for the "punk neighborhood kids." It was Ben, the restaurant owner's son. Ben seemed like he was always looking for a chance like this—a chance to catch us in the act of some nefarious scheme. So we did what we'd always done. We ran. As the light swept across the pavement, Steve and I made a beeline for a pile of wooden pallets in the alley, ducking behind them as fast as we could.

We did our best to peer through the cracks of the cheap pine, but there was no clear view of Ben or of the pile of ice. As we sat still behind our wooden fortress, he exited the car just as the unmistakable sound of the plastic bottle finally reaching its threshold echoed through the corridor of cement and bricks.

Though no physical damage was done (we never intended to be destructive), our little experiment nonetheless came with consequences. Fifty hours of community service later, everything changed for me—I just didn't know it yet. I served those fifty hours at the church I had attended since before first grade. It was the church where I had prayed a hundred—maybe a thousand—times for Jesus to forgive me and come back into my heart, because I was sure He had left. It was the church where I heard my dad's story of transformation from a pagan-like hippie (and all that comes with it) to a follower of Jesus. It was the church that had performed so much to teach me about who Jesus was. But I had not yet learned how to follow Him; I had not yet learned to be His disciple. I had memorized Scripture, done drama skits on stage for the pastor's messages, and participated in every Vacation Bible School they had. But it was in those fifty hours of swinging hammers, hanging drywall, and painting that I finally caught what was being taught. I experienced firsthand the slow-to-anger attitude of Dale and Doug when mistakes were made. I discovered compassion when Mike had to teach an easily distracted teenager how to use a drill. I encountered the hospitality of God through James, who made a killer gumbo that I have yet to duplicate. What was being said and sung about and sermonized just didn't stick until I was shoulder to shoulder with the people of my church...outside the rows of the sanctuary on a Sunday morning.

That's when everything changed. Soon I began to look for more opportunities like the one I was required to do. I started to seek out those who would pour into me (like Ben), and soon enough, those who I could pour into. And it wasn't until I wrote these very words that I recognized this as one of the most significant moments in my life as a follower of Jesus. Years after the "Works Bomb" incident, after serving in student ministry as a pastor, people would ask how it was that, with my background (it was labeled as dysfunctional back then), I came out not just okay, but "good." I always shrugged my shoulders and just said, "God must have been up to something." He was up to something alright. Those fifty hours took what I had vaguely paid attention to and translated it into action. Compassion, patience, thankfulness, joy, self-control, kindness, wisdom and understanding were all being embodied while I served my time. Those fifty hours showed me that obedience to Christ is not taught in a classroom or learned in a pew—it's taught in relationships with those who have been shown by others (who were shown by others). It's imparted and passed on through everyday encounters with people who embody the abundant life promised in Christ and then share it with others.

That's how Jesus intended it to be.
That's how Jesus did it.
And that's how He told us to do it.

Jesus Could Have Done Anything

Have you ever thought about how Jesus could have done it? What Jesus could have done during His lifetime? Jesus could have done anything. Think about that for a second. If you were Jesus and had three years to fulfill your mission, what would you do?

Scott recently asked a group of students that same question. Jesus had three years and could have done anything. What would they as students do? One proposed ending world hunger (perhaps multiplying on a global scale, the feeding of the 5,000). Another said cure the world of all diseases—line up the ill, sick and lame. It would have been a busy three years, but maybe it could have been done; after all, this is Jesus we are talking about!

Pretty good answers.

Scott had some fun answers about what he would do if he were Jesus. He gets amped up by the idea of renting out Wrigley Field in Chicago. Actually, he's not a Cubs fan, so Busch Stadium in St. Louis is more likely. You get the idea, big stadium with state-of-the-art AV systems.

Open the event with Stryper, the '80s Christian metal band on a reunion tour (or maybe Kanye West or Justin Bieber...or whatever celebrity Christian convert is making headlines). After the performance, but with music still playing, comes the dramatic entrance. As Jesus, Scott would call down rain from heaven, a downpour illuminated with a synchronized mass-scale light show. Actually, the rain falls only in the Olympic-sized pool in the middle of the stadium. Next is the Sermon on the Mount, now in stereo surround and with an interactive LED experience that the band U2 would be jealous of. As the sermon wraps up with the parable of the foolish builder, Scott walks on the water of the now full pool.

Mic float...

A supernatural mic drop doesn't drop...it levitates and then ascends into heaven.

"And 50,000 were added to their number that day,[3]" baptized in the miraculously filled pool!

Over the top?

Is it?

Okay, there might be some exaggerations, and they might border on sacrilege. Yet when you put some of those aside, the idea is not that far-fetched from what we would do. In fact, it's not that far-fetched from what has become the trend for the way many Christians in the US now gather for worship.

Jesus could have done anything.

If you were Jesus, what would you do?

Would you...

Start as many churches as you could as fast as you could?

Start networks of churches that spread across regions, even countries?

Fill as many 20,000-seat auditoriums as you could find and broadcast the best preaching and teaching?

Work with the politicians and lawmakers to get back to a moral and upright society, allying groups of young and diverse crowds to march through the streets of all the major cities from LA to DC?

Use mass media to get the message out—social media, viral videos, books, podcasts, vodcasts, or TED Talks? Could you imagine the TED Talks if you were Jesus? If you, as Jesus, had a YouTube channel, it would fund ministry for decades!

Most versions of what we would do are likely amped up, multiplied, and magnified versions of what we already do. Typically our answers are just bigger and better versions of our current efforts. With our resources and Jesus' talent, why wouldn't we do all of that? Maybe because Jesus didn't.

Jesus didn't build a bigger or better building of worship. He could have made a temple that would make Disney World look like a parking lot carnival. And, unlike the "great" kings, pharaohs, emperors, and empires of the world, He would have done it without enslaving people.

He could have performed a miracle a minute. Jesus did perform powerful miracles that got a lot of people's attention. His signs and wonders moved people and stirred up belief, yet Jesus didn't make His miracles the center of His mission.

Jesus could have set up a soapbox in the middle of the temple courts. Jesus delivered powerful sermons that did attract crowds. Those crowds often heard words so challenging that they dispersed. And when they didn't dissipate, Jesus did His best to pull away and get away, even getting on boats to go to the other side of a sea.

He could have started a coalition with the political powers and cultural influencers. Jesus did talk with the elites, but it was often in opposition and with harsh criticism. When He had a chance to rub shoulders with the elite of society, He instead chose to be associated with the outsiders and undignified.

When it comes to creating some sort of social movement, Jesus could have united the faction groups of people in Israel at the time. They had a compelling common cause: freedom from Roman oppression. Yet outside of the influential religious puppet rulers (scribes and Pharisees), we hear nothing about any efforts of unification. Jesus could have assembled a group of collaborative, innovative community developers together and reformed all of Jerusalem. With Jesus' relational skills alone, He could have certainly created an activist (even zealot) movement against any number of issues, including oppressive taxes, greedy lawmakers, narcissistic rulers, systemic injustice...

Jesus could have participated in public debates about Scripture, given well reasoned arguments and proofs. Remember, when Jesus was twelve years old (just twelve), He made quite the impression on the teachers in the temple court. Right then and there, He could have leveraged His prodigy status and built a following. Instead, Jesus returned to be with His parents.

He could have set up a nice seminary overlooking the Sea of Galilee, taken resumes and applications for the best and the brightest—the rock stars and the credentialed, those who had proven themselves with effectiveness and results. Instead, He chose the uneducated and ordinary.

Jesus had three years and, in that time, what He did was not a lot like what we would do. It's not even a lot like what we actually do. He could have done anything. What He did was:

Simple.
Small.
Slow.
Sustainable.

What Jesus did was relational and intentional. He poured His life into 12 people.

Jesus spent the majority of His time, energy and effort during His ministry with 12 people. With the guidance of the Father, Jesus chose 12 people that would start as learners and become friends. Twelve ordinary but curious people. What Jesus did was not extravagant or enormous, it wasn't expedited or expensive. In the centuries since

Jesus walked this earth, these people would go on to be called the twelve disciples. They would become icons of the church, saints, and spiritual giants (well, almost all of them). Let's not forget, however, that these 12 (Peter; Andrew; James; John; Philip; Bartholomew; Matthew; Thomas; James, son of Alphaeus; Simon (the Zealot); Judas, son of James; and Judas Iscariot) started their journey in the same place everyone does: with an invitation to be loved by Jesus and to love others the same.

What Jesus did was simple. It was small, it was slow, and it didn't require a capital campaign—it was sustainable.

Jesus found 12.

Questions for Reflection and Discussion

1. If you were Jesus and had three years to fulfill your mission, what would you do?
2. How would you describe Jesus' ministry to someone?
3. What makes Jesus' strategy sustainable?

2

Confronting the Brutal Fact

"Strictly speaking one ought to
say that the Church is always in a
state of crisis and that its greatest
shortcoming is that it is only
occasionally aware of it."

–*ALAN HIRSH, THE FORGOTTEN WAYS*

CHAPTER 2

1, 2, 3, 4...

The look on Sean's face, and the pit left in my stomach from what he said, is something hard to forget. It was a typical Wednesday night at the church where, for a few years, I had been the director of student ministry at a multi-site church. By all accounts, we were successful. We were doing back-to-back services for middle school and high school students. The band and tech was composed of mostly high school students with a few adult leaders keeping things from getting too out of whack. While one group was meeting for worship, another was playing dodge ball in the basement and meeting in small groups. We had tons of adults leading those activities and small groups for over 150 students. At least, that was the size of our ministry at the beginning of the ministry year, when excitement was high and efforts for invitations were numerous. But this day was not quite like those Wednesdays in the fall.

Students trickled into the dark room with rows of chairs facing the bright and colorful illuminated stage. The band had practiced for hours. I had rehearsed my message at least twice and made the necessary revisions. We had done the run-through of the service and had the timing down pretty tight. Well, tight enough. Per usual, I stood at the back of the room praying, processing final thoughts, and pushing back on the thing that was ever present. The thing that I would be asked about Thursday morning in a weekly email. The THING that had begun to seem like the biggest voice as to what success or "Kingdom impact" or value or worth or identity hinged on. I could glance around the room and have an accurate estimation as to how many chairs had students planted in them. Regardless, I started counting. My eyes scanned back and forth through the rows checking to see if some prepubescent sixth-grade boy was tucked in front of an "Andre the Giant" eighth grader. It wasn't easy counting... two students headed for the bathroom...three came in late...one moved seats...twice. So I counted again. I hated what I was doing. I probably counted a third time.

Someone is always counting. Counting has become a hallmark of the church in the US. The church loves to count.

It was after the service that Sean said what he said. After I had the student count ingrained in my head. A number that, in my mind, was far less than acceptable. A number that had me say in my "Minnesota nice" passive-aggressive way, "Was there some event at school tonight?" It was less direct than what I had said from the stage in prior weeks, which was "It's your job to know why your friends and classmates aren't here." I continued to direct my inquiry to the few students that were helping me stack chairs. "Man, there was like no one here this week."

Something must have built up in Sean, something unsettling and maybe even wounding.

With nearly no hesitation he said, *"We're* here."

The comment came with a slightly puzzled look on his face, as if to say, *Don't we count? Don't we matter?"* What I heard in my heart as I read his eyes was, *Are numbers all that matters to you, Jake? Is that what this is all about?* Of course it wasn't. At least that's what I told myself in the moment. That's what I told myself in the next minutes as I backpedaled and stammered through my justification for being so concerned about the predictable dip in participation in our program. I disingenuously attempted to vision cast about how it wasn't about the numbers, that our mission was about helping students find their way to God, and how our efforts were doing just that. And that's why we needed to invite...

And then I apologized.

I stopped counting that week. I gave a rough estimate instead. The numbers in the spreadsheet didn't change much...because I eventually stopped recording them. The numbers guy taking account of every service at every campus across all ages eventually caught on and just went with the trends. What DID change was my focus. Don't get me wrong, I loved what we were doing; I loved the productions, loved to get on stage and teach and speak. Scott and I were pretty good at manufacturing the numbers. By all conventional metrics, we were successful. New students were coming every week. We had adult leaders who loved to serve (and there was no shortage of them). We had student-led ministry teams of arts, tech, and setup/teardown.

We had dodgeball in the unfinished basement and were the reigning champs of the annual church-wide tournament for nearly half a decade. Other campuses were coming to check out what we were doing to figure out why it was working. We could bust our tails to craft and plan a worship service and engaging activities that would pack our spaces, but Sean's words revealed something that had gone unnoticed and unaddressed for too long. We had traded pouring into the relationships in front of us for the potential of progress and growth ahead of us.

Here is the kicker. At least for Scott and me, what we were doing back then was and is the pinnacle of spiritual experience for many of those students. From time to time, we will connect with one of those individuals from that era, and they will inevitably bring up the good old days of that student ministry. Every spiritual encounter is measured against that time (as if our program was a really good restaurant to which all others are compared). We were very successful at making spiritual consumers. And those consumers were thoroughly ill-informed about the Just 12 model of Jesus. It's impossible to really know the actual numbers of followers of Jesus today (let alone those connected to a church). We shudder to even venture a guess. We have a haunting question as to the spiritual trajectory of the masses whose attention we worked so hard to gain and hold. Please don't mishear this. Certainly God worked good in the lives of many, many of those students. And some of their stories we will not know this side of eternity. We are also certain, however, that only a handful of those students received a clear message about what it means to join Jesus in living His message and mission.

As for me, in twenty-plus years of ministry, I was never evaluated or reviewed for how I was doing making disciples. Scott said the same about his fifteen years on staff at the church where we served together. Instead, it was about the turnout at events, the percentage growth of baptisms, budgets, and spending, or how many more people came this year than last. The focus was rarely Jesus-modeled discipleship. A Jesus-model strategy just wasn't as "productive." Unfortunately, like many vocational ministry jobs, expectations were outcome-oriented. The growth and maintenance of the organization took precedent. Anything else was viewed as distracting. Time spent consistently and regularly pouring into individuals has little value if it cannot be tied to measurable organizational metrics. I have served in five different churches, from mainline to nondenominational, church plant to multi-site. None of those roles explicitly expected that I would be making disciples through constant and intentional relationship building. Any encouragement for consistent and intentional relationship building was, again, primarily focused on organizational growth and maintenance. In other words, any person on the receiving end of relational investment needed to be identified as a potential contributor (volunteer or donor). Efforts to build relationships with discipleship as the focus were quickly overshadowed by more visible and easily quantifiable-driven activities.

Jesus Christ: Super Pastor

It's interesting to contemplate how Jesus would have fared as a pastor in the "church as a business" model we have so wholeheartedly come to accept. The standards held by most churches for what pastors should be doing and how much they should be doing it would likely lead to Jesus being let go or transitioned out of most churches today. Our outcomes-oriented hustle culture would have little tolerance for some of the ways Jesus practiced ministry. Jesus spent a disproportionate amount of time on retreat away from His public ministry. He walked *away* from crowds wanting more of His teaching and healing. He hung out with a number of people with questionable reputations. His attention seemed overwhelmingly one-sided toward those on the margins of society. He was constantly challenging the status quo, on all sides. He broke all sorts of traditions and pushed against the sentimentalities of religious life. And He spent the majority of His time with the same twelve people.

How do you think Jesus would do on staff at the churches you know of? Could He cut it? Would He have the capacity for the demanding schedule and expectations? Would His vision sustain the attention of the entertainment-hungry crowds? Would He play by the rules to appease the influential people sustaining the overhead? Would He be respectful and tactful enough about the history of the church? Would He flip over the wrong tables in the lobby? Let's face it, from what we see Jesus doing, we don't envision Him scrutinizing the spreadsheets, HR policies, or year-end giving. He didn't have a ten-year strategy. His three-year plan of "I'm leaving, it's your turn" wouldn't hit the growth and multiplication goals, wouldn't fit the brand and would be a marketing nightmare for most churches today.

Jesus didn't have the qualifications and credentials to meet many of the standards and expectations we aspire to be filled in our churches today. He didn't have the right credentials in His day, either. And at the end of His early ministry the only thing Jesus had to show for his efforts was a group of people He had poured into. Well, that and a death-conquering, ressurected body with the visible wounds of the cross.

Discipled disciple makers and new life were Jesus' credentials. You'd think that would be enough. This may be a bold statement, but consider the exponential decline of Christianity in our time. Jesus' credentials are no longer the measure of success in the church of the US. If they were, we would have long ago noticed and responded.

We have no shortage of stats highlighting the downward trends of Christianity in the U.S.

- Around World War II, 75% of America attended a church on Sunday morning. That number is quickly declining to just 15% (Outreach Magazine).[4]

- Half of self-identified Christians and more than half of churched adults overall admit that people they know are tired of the usual type of church experience. (Barna 2020)[5] And this is before the COVID-19 virus changed everything.

- During the Great Depression giving to churches was at 3.3% of people's income. Today it hovers around 2.5% (NPSource 2018).[6]

- 17% of Americans say they NEVER attend religious services, up from 11% a decade ago. A decline in Christian affiliation and church attendance continues to drop with each emerging generation (Pew).[7]

- The alarming 59% church dropout rate of young adults (2011) has now climbed to 64% (Barna).[8]

- In a recent study, only 6% of America has a Bible-centered worldview (CRC).[9]

More and more, we are seeing fewer and fewer people interested in identifying with the Christian faith. Although it goes against what many pastors and church communities believe, we are just not seeing disciples making disciples as a result of all the "church" efforts. Perhaps this is why more international missionaries are now being sent into the US than any other country in the world (Gospel Coalition).[10]

We agree with those who say that this narrative is ripe for the kingdom; that the good news has fertile ground. Yet even with a sense of urgency of those paying attention, there seems to be no focus on the symptoms behind the stats. At best this focus is on a desire to treat the symptoms, and at worst it is using the symptoms as an excuse to be complacent. Many theories exist as to what's to blame for the decline.

Could it be...

> ...the erosion of Judeo-Christian morals and ethics?
> ...the lack of resources due to the drop in generosity towards churches?
> ...the scandals of the church over abuses of power?

We could give some lengthy rebuttals to each of these. After all, Christian morals and ethics in America have seen a steady decline over the last 100 years, but the church has never needed a moral culture in order to thrive. Generosity towards the institution of the church has declined, but we now have more access and support to information, technology, accountability, networks, training, coaching and resources than can be absorbed in 100 lifetimes. And certainly the abuses of power across nearly every Christian denomination are atrocious and damning (and those are just the ones we know of). But these issues are antithetical to the Jesus mission and message, not representative. They often cause people to be hungry and desperate for a leadership and movement that embodies the very message of the cross.

These issues are not to blame for the spiritual decline we are facing. None of those are the cause; they are symptoms. They are the result of the lack of disciples making disciples. The lack of disciple-making disciples is primarily a result of a faithful pursuit of misguided and misplaced—or maybe just overused and outdated—strategies.

We believe that the biggest contributor to the spiritual decline in America rests primarily on the lack of participation of everyday followers of Jesus to be disciple makers.

The word discipleship (disciple and disciple-maker) is a "churchy" word. It's not a word that has much use outside religious contexts. Still, there aren't many words that serve as a substitute. Apprentice, mentee, friend, learner, student or padawan (for you Star Wars fans) are insufficient on their own. And using half a dozen words to communicate Jesus' relationship model and philosophy isn't very practical. Communicating how Jesus invested in relationships should be approachable for everyone. Hopefully those of you who are unfamiliar with this language don't get hung up on it for too long, and any familiarity does not become a blinder to possibilities outside what you already know. The values, intentionality and prioritization that Jesus had in His relationships havent translated easily to our times. So, "discipleship" it is.

Jesus' primary plan, demonstrated in His ministry and commanded in His commission, is that His disciples would be disciple makers. We have twisted that into getting people to show up at religious centers to consume religious goods and services, delivered by religious professionals who petition for provisions to keep the whole thing running and in some cases expanding. This is a far cry from those first disciples of Jesus who left everything and risked everything to tell the world they encountered the the one who was crucified then resurreced and gave us the way to new and eternal life.

No, the collective scorecard across the U.S. is not one of Kingdom success. Although the current system of churches in the U.S. has some positive gains, some big losses have also been ignored, forgotten or, even worse yet, spun. Unfortunately, Scott and I have story after story of pastors, volunteers and faithful churchgoers that have been pushed out, fired and shut down because the organizations to which they gave their all were obsessed with manufacturing and maintaining church growth.

Maybe those disenfranchised, disenchanted and disinterested in the church don't have a technical or theological term for it. While we church folks preach the importance of community (i.e., "you need to come to church"), others see a disconnect between the message and the method, a disintegration between preaching and practice. People sense that what little they do know of discipleship and following after Jesus isn't often demonstrated in the church or by the church. We have told the world that there is more to life than living for the weekend, but that is exactly how Christians function.

A few years ago, Christian author Jim Henderson traveled the United States visiting all kinds of churches with Matt Casper, an atheist. In the book written about their experiences, Jim comments about the devastating question Casper posed over and over again throughout their travels. Casper's question gets to the heart of the problem. Jim recalls what Casper saw and experienced over and over again, "with big budgets and no budgets, in large stadiums and in small buildings.

The same format repeated itself regardless of the setting." In nearly every instance, at some point Casper would ask, "Is this what Jesus told you guys to do?" At the end of the visits, after a year of seeing nearly every style and denomination of church, Casper was confused. Confused that churches invest millions of dollars and countless hours doing church completely differently than what they described in the Bible. Jim writes, "Casper simply could not imagine Jesus telling his followers that the most important thing they should do is holding church services. And yet this was the only logical conclusion he was able to come to based on what he'd observed."[11] Why is the question that is so clear for an atheist not also a glaring confrontation for many of us followers of Jesus? What we do when we do church is not what Jesus told us to do.

What Can We Do About It?

It appears that glimpses of awareness of everything we have just described do exist, even if the awareness is subconscious for some. The bigger and more important question is whether or not we are going to do something other than what we are currently doing. Our current systems are perfectly equipped to produce what they are currently producing.

Option 1: Do nothing & ride it out

For some, the thought of doing anything sounds exhausting. Retirement benefits are on the line, and livelihoods are at stake. The risks might just be too high.

Option 2: Change the gathering

This seems to be the preferred method of just about everyone who is concerned about the decline. The responses are tweaks to worship services or weekend programming, offering more options and more times (with the aid of technology), all in the hopes of seeing a rise in attendance or a spike in engagement (or in many cases avoiding the decline). It's adding new songs or taking out old ones. It's starting a new emerging generation service, online service or daily social media posts. It's hiring younger or more diverse staff or changing the length of the service. In times when weekend gatherings have been limited because of global health crises, the response has been much of the same: changing the delivery methods and environments for the gatherings. There is no shortage of ideas and options. The results of successful changes are typically some growth and engagement, but they are often short-lived. It's only a matter of time before the need for another tweak comes along.

Option 3: Serial Multiplication

More, more and more (of the same). The idea of multiplication stresses outpacing the decline of Christianity by multiplying new and more churches (whose focus is still primarily on weekend gatherings). It's typically a modified version of the above strategy but with the tweaks coming on a grander scale. It's the same strategy at a macro level. It's duplicating and multiplying the efforts of those churches with some level of success with attendance and financial growth. How is it that we think multiplying more of what's not working is going to yield better results? It's almost as if we believe we can help America consume its way into discipleship and the Kingdom. What is baffling is how far we've moved away from the simple strategy that Jesus employed and passed on to the disciples and to us.

A healthy church will multiply and duplicate, but duplication and multiplication does not equal health. Cancer and viruses often multiply at a ravenous rate, yet no one thinks cancer is a sign of health.

Another Option: A Return to the Original Strategy

Jesus had 12.

Just 12.

Jesus had 12 people that received the majority of his time, energy, and relational investment. Just 12, that He made the priority for modeling what a life lived in His ways would look like.

What if we had just 12?

We are not saying to stop gathering for worship, but what if the strategy was flipped? What would happen if we decreased the investment of time and energy (and money) on productions and programs we hope will make people into disciples, and instead increased our focus on just 12 people—intentionally seeking to make disciples in the way Jesus demonstrated? This isn't just a challenge for pastor types. This is for every follower of Jesus to intentionally choose 12 people they sense God is directing them toward. Just 12 is a challenge for each of us to find 12 people who will receive the majority of our energies and resources.

Just 12.

Twelve people may feel like a lot. It would be, and will be, if you try to keep doing the manufactured church thing at the same time in the same ways. You'll not have time. You won't make time. You'll try to disciple everyone and end up discipling no one. Through human efforts, you'll manufacture some disciple-like results but miss the disciple-making way of Jesus. We are becoming more convinced everyday that Jesus wasn't talking only about adopting sentiment and feelings that reflected the heart of His commands; He expects us to imitate the actions He modeled in those commands. What if when Jesus said to His followers, "A new command I give you, to love others...as I have loved you[12]" and "as the father sent me I send you[13]" and "Go and make disciples,[14]" He intended for us to adopt His methods and strategy? What if Jesus wants us to follow His model for morality AND His model of mission?

Questions for Reflection and Discussion

1. America is in an exponential spiritual decline. Why do you think this is?

2. What has your church experience been like?

3. Discuss the four options. In your opinion, which do you think is the best?

3

Crowds

"Then Jesus dismissed the crowds…"

–*Matt. 13:36*

3

THE ORIGINAL STRATEGY IN AFRICA, INDIA, CHINA... AND AMERICA TOO?

"I came to America to learn how to do ministry."

Sounds like a smart thing to do. Lots of people all over the world seek education and training in the U.S. What was strange for me about these words is what was said right before them. It was early on in my graduate work at Wheaton College. Our class had been divided into groups to share about our experiences making disciples. Most everyone in my group shared about one or two relationships that over the years yielded "disciple-like" results. Mainly it was a person we had influenced who, in almost every case, followed closely in our footsteps and pursued ministry in some form or another.

When Tariku shared about his time at a university in Ethiopia, we were awestruck by how seemingly ignorant he was to the uniqueness and power of his story. Tariku began with how he and a few of his friends each started meeting with two other students over a semester, teaching them about Jesus, how to study the Bible, and how to start talking to others about their faith. Then he told how over the next semester those students each started doing the same with two additional students. He continued on about how over the next couple of semesters this practice held strong, and that in a few short years the numbers had grown to over 150 students being discipled in the ways of Jesus.

When Tariku said he needed to come to Wheaton College "to learn how to do ministry," the rest of us looked at one another wide-eyed. Someone spoke up and said, "Tariku, you should be at the front of the class teaching us! Not the other way around. We need to be learning from you!"

It had never occurred to Tariku that he was doing the very thing we all were desperate to learn (and maybe more so that we needed to unlearn what we were doing). The U.S. strategy for disciple-making did not look like what he and his friends had started. Certainly what he was learning in our program would be put to great use for his ministry. Nonetheless, Tariku's story highlights just how skewed our vision for making disciples has become. Today, Christianity is blossoming in many parts of the world because the simple strategy of Jesus is prioritized.

China

Ying Kai and his wife, Grace, are most commonly referred to as church planters. It is what they did as missionaries to Eastern Asia for many years. In the year 2000, they felt led to start churches in China. Prior to 2000, Ying would have been considered a pretty successful church planter. He had seen many people come to faith and had started several churches. But a conviction and overwhelming heart to reach over 20 million people caused him to re-engage the final command of Jesus to live as disciple makers. It was from that re-engagement with Christ's Great Commission and lots of prayer that a Jesus-molded strategy emerged, called Train for Trainers, or T4T. Ying says that in the middle of the night he came to a realization that changed everything. Recounting that night he reflected, "We've known the Great Commission since we were children, we memorized this passage of Scripture, and we were even able to sing it in a song. But...we discovered that we had never really followed His Great Commission." This came after years of successful church planting.

The results of Ying and Grace's efforts sound almost mythical. They had a goal of reaching 18,000 new people with the message of Jesus and to start 200 new churches. Within just 18 months, they had already surpassed that goal. Since then, they have seen similar surges from those who have taken up the effort of getting back to the basics of Jesus' strategy—with thousands of new believers in places from India to Ukraine.

The T4T discipleship strategy is labeled as a church multiplication movement because thousands of churches have been started with a huge influx of followers of Jesus engaging in their faith. However, at its core, what Ying and Grace have been champions of is Jesus-modeled disciple-making.

I had a chance to listen and speak to Ying over a video conference call, where he described in person much of what I shared above. I asked him, "Why is this model not effective in the U.S.?"

Ying had apparently been asked this a lot, for he was ready with a response. "America is too impatient and too focused on growth. They are looking for something that will be big right away and can be added to what they already do. This model (T4T), much like the Jesus model, is about starting small, and it's almost all that you do."

Discipleship as Ying describes it works to fulfill the Great Commission and apparently to fill churches and, yes, to start movements; but it was and is primarily about making disciples as Jesus modeled it. T4T is a return to the simple, small, slow and sustainable.

Iran

This strong adherence to a Jesus-modeled form of discipleship is taking hold in other places too. The 2019 documentary *Sheep Among Wolves, Volume II* followed the underground Christian movement in Iran.

The film highlights how the church (in Iran) owns no buildings, has no centralized leadership and is spearheaded primarily by women. And the strategy of those women, who are experiencing incredible joy even in the face of persecution, is not planting churches but disciple-making. The documentary is powerful and moving and worth watching. It is convicting, too. The women's commitment to faith and unwavering surrender to Jesus and His mission and methods pushes us to consider how comfortable we have become with consumerist and spectator faith.

These stories and others like them plague us with a question:

If the basic Jesus-modeled form of discipleship is working in other places, why are we not making it the central strategy in our churches? It's working in places where there is no lack of evil. One might make a case that it's thriving in some of the most oppressive environments our world can muster. It worked through an untrained college student in Ethiopia. It's working for the women who are offering themselves as living sacrifices, fully aware of the dangers of following Jesus. It worked for the successful church planter in China and changed his whole strategy. If we are looking for what will have the greatest impact on the spiritual landscape in America, why are we looking beyond what Jesus said? Why is the central part of our strategy anything but disciple-making?

When we get outside of the U.S., we discover that Christianity is not in decline in the rest of the world; it is growing. The good news is still good news, and when it's shared and cultivated in a Jesus-modeled form of discipleship, it thrives. The key to exponential growth is not serial multiplication of what we in the U.S. are currently doing, it's returning to the basic model of discipleship displayed and commissioned by Jesus. Some might have us believe that the key is more churches, and that we should focus our energies there. This line of thinking seems to make church planting and discipleship interchangeable. The modern methods of church planting and the early church form of discipleship are not interchangeable. There very well may be cases where Jesus-modeled discipleship is the main driver behind church planting, and thus the two ideas become inseparable. They are related and interconnected, but they are not synonymous. In the countries and places where discipleship is the focus, a church multiplication movement exists. But the movements are not energized by church planting efforts. Rather, they are built on and driven by disciple-making efforts. Disciples making disciples leads to church multiplication, and not the other way around. Where church multiplication is the focus, there are some disciples; but they lack the commitment and zeal found in places like China and Iran. They also lack the intensity and intentionality of active disciple-making.

It is a disservice to ordinary, everyday followers of Jesus to suggest that church program attendance, volunteer work or even being part of starting a church are the same things as participation in disciple-making. Exponential growth comes not when a few high-level achievers and leaders get together and collaborate to achieve something magnificent; it happens when everyday followers of Jesus do what Jesus said. Exponential is what happens when everyone that follows Jesus participates in His mandate. Exponential is the result of no one being excluded on either side of the conversion equation. Exponential is eliminating the equations and focusing on the relational strategy that Jesus modeled.

The T4T philosophy is that every believer needs to participate in disciple-making, even the newest of believers. Ying said this model rarely works in America, not because the model is ineffective, but because the U.S. strategies and approaches to church are focused on other priorities.

Jesus regularly dismissed the crowds in favor of pouring into His twelve. Churches in the U.S. don't like to dismiss the crowds. We covet the crowds. The U.S. seems to believe that a movement happens in the crowds. What we learn through Jesus' form of discipleship, in the early church, both in many of the Jesus movements throughout history, is that movement happens as we go throughout our days pouring into those God has called us to reach, showing them in our action and words what it means to live a life obedient to our Rescuer. This way may not be as pretty or fast or prestigious, but it's the way Jesus has called us to. Can we trust Him enough to let go of our latest schemes and grand visions and instead reconnect and re-engage with the strategy He has given since the very beginning?

The Jesus movement is growing. The lowest common denominator is nothing more and nothing less than disciple-making.

Questions for Reflection and Discussion

1. Why do you think America has not grasped disciple-making like some other countries?
2. What makes America's current church growth strategy compelling for so many?

4

What do you say discipleship is?

> "Surely the challenge for the church today is to be taken captive by the agenda of Jesus, rather than seeking to mold him to fit our agendas, no matter how noble they might be."
>
> –*Michael Frost, ReJesus: A Wild Messiah for a Missional Church*

CHAPTER 4

DEFINITIONS

Scott once attended a well-known church leadership conference. It was like most other conferences with several big name keynote speakers, a few popular authors and leaders of the fastest growing churches, and some breakouts for specific topics. Of course, there was also a theme that was a banner for all the headline communicators were given a theme to follow. This particular topic, as was trendy at the time, was discipleship.

Most of the content at the conference was helpful, and the presenters were enthusiastic. All sorts of definitions of discipleship were also being offered. It seemed that each communicator was customizing a definition of discipleship to fit their preferences, experiences and context. The voices for church planting and church growth said discipleship is about leadership apprenticing and reproduction. The justice-oriented voices said it's about building relationships through community development and advocacy by helping the poor and under-resourced.

The programmatic voices said it was providing groups, studies and experiences that help build a like-minded community with deep knowledge and understanding. The missional camp said it's getting into the neighborhood and talking over fences and having people around the table. Most of us, it seems, interchange our preferences and definitions. Although Scott and I agree that discipleship is fluid and can and should be adapted to fit our circumstances, we also think a basic understanding of discipleship can easily be agreed upon. What discipleship is, in our opinion, is pretty clear. Yet how discipleship plays out has some fluidity and very well might include many aspects of the ideas listed above.

We don't want to pretend that we have all the right answers, but we do think the right answer about discipleship is a lot more clear and a lot less complicated than many make it out to be.

Discipling is loving our 12 like Jesus loved His.

Disciple-making is teaching those 12 how to do the same.

This definition doesn't exclude any practices or preferences. At the same time, it allows each and every follower of Jesus to approach every relationship with the same posture. It's the posture of Jesus—an others-focused, self-sacrificial love that is free of personal or corporate agenda. Because each of us has a unique context and calling (Jesus was called to the lost sheep of Israel), specific practices may take on different forms; but each will be rooted in a model that is clearly traced back to the Jesus way.

The chapters that follow focus on how to find our 12, as well as the implications this definition of discipleship presses on us. These practices transcend preferences. No matter the context or relationship dynamic (boss, coworker, child, spouse, parent, etc.), we can approach everyone in a similar and simple manner.

Before we start, we do need to be clear that 12 is not a requirement. Although 12 has some historical and theological implications, it also has some practical ones. The choosing of 12 by Jesus and the intentionality of putting the majority of His energies into these relationships speaks to powerful dynamics we believe are part of the model we are meant to imitate. Those dynamics are about intimacy and inclusion. All of us have only so much bandwidth for intimacy and inclusion. For some of us, our capacities may accommodate only a few. It's unlikely anyone could have many more than 12. More than 12 will leave us and our relationships stretched thin. If we attempt to love more than 12, we'll likely not love like Jesus did. The bottom line is that Just 12 is a stark contrast to the mass-scaled productions and programming on which we've come to rely. And, as we have established, it's not what we see in the model of Jesus.

The next several chapters explore how each of us can select our 12 and how practices of serving, socializing, sharing, sending and soul-refueling reorient us to the model that sparked the Jesus movement. Behind these practices are actionable values that we see evident in the biblical narratives about Jesus. They are also evident in the early church that carried the mission forward and the many movements that have found themselves caught up in the Jesus movement.

Radical Dependency – Jesus had an unwavering commitment to hear from the Spirit of God through prayer, solitude, Scripture and community. This is the root of His identity and the source of power and authority He carried into the world. Jesus only did that which He saw the Father doing, and He regularly spent time surrendering His own will to the will of the Father.

Uncommon Inclusion – Jesus reached across divides of gender, religion, politics, status, wealth and more. His approach to befriending others was rooted in seeing and treating every person as an invaluable creation of the Father.

Engaging Presence – Jesus had an undistracted relational focus that could discern the work of God in each person, encounter and circumstance. Wherever Jesus went, He was fully present, looking and listening to the lives of the people who were with Him.

Unguarded Vulnerability – Jesus was authentic and disarmed in communicating His experiences, emotions and intentions. Like the unveiling of the Kingdom throughout Scripture, Jesus embodies the message of a God who wants to be known by and partner with His creation.

Willful Humility – Jesus chose humility before He even entered our existence. It is humility that we are commanded to imitate.[14] Ultimately Jesus surrenders His divine rights and equalities for the sake of bringing those He loves into a right and restored relationship with God and all of creation. In His daily existence, Jesus dismantled the hierarchies and positioning so prevalent in our world.

These actionable values form, inform and reform us as followers of Jesus and disciple makers. With the power of the Spirit they also become tools to transform us more and more into the image of Christ. They help us embody the values of Jesus and His mission so that any words we share, with either skeptics or believers, will be congruent with who we are trying to become in Jesus.

Questions for Reflection and Discussion

1. How would you define discipleship?
2. Who do you know that excels at disciple-making?

5

Select your 12

"Truly successful decision-
making relies on a balance
between deliberate and
instinctive thinking."

–MALCOLM GLADWELL

CHAPTER 5

UP ALL NIGHT

On that dreadful night that began the wrongful imprisonment, torture and execution of the Messiah, Jesus could be found in a garden of olive trees just outside the city. It was a place where He often went to pray with His disciples. On this particular occurrence, He spent the whole night in prayer. His disciples, unable to endure the darkness and cold, huddled together against a tree and fell asleep, unaware of the coming doom that awaited their friend and Lord.

It's one of only two times we are told that Jesus spent the whole night in prayer. In this instance, He did so only before the most grueling and trying moments of his life. Do you know the only other recorded time that He prayed all night? In the four narratives written about His life, only one other all-night prayer vigil is mentioned. Sure, Jesus would wake early to seek time with the Father, but all-nighters of prayer? It seems the most pivotal moments called for a certain level of dedication, commitment and maybe even desperation.

The other time was the night before He chose His 12.

For Jesus, the 12 people He would pour His life into were of utmost importance. These 12 humans would carry His message and mission to the world for the rest of this age (until the reconciliation and fulfillment of all things). Though they were unaware of it, there were the flawed and ordinary people who would be invited to discover a fully dependent, radically inclusive, intensely present, astonishingly vulnerable God who would entrust them to live what Jesus mandated and modeled. They would be included in the full life that Jesus came to give and tasked with proclaiming the never-diminishing life that comes from resting and trusting the creator and sustainer of all things.

If discipleship is about inviting and including others in the ways of Jesus—at least the ways we fumble to understand and fumble even more to follow—we need to be like Jesus and take seriously those whom we are going to invite and include. This, too, is counterintuitive in light of our modern practices of church ministry. We leave to circumstances how our small groups are formed or who we sit next to in church or who we decide to share our faith journey with. We kind of "take it as it comes." Yet God is not a God of coincidence. He is a God of great intentionality, so He will certainly use what seems random to bring us and others into a life under His rule and rescue. At the same time, we cannot take lightly His tremendous consideration and concern about His 12. Our 12, the 12 we will commit to invest the greatest portion of our energies and time, should be worked out with fear and trembling. Just as we work out our own salvation, we should take seriously the lives of those we seek to usher into and lead through new creation.

Imagine Jesus heading up a mountain with a sense that His ministry is now moving into partnership with His followers. It's uncertain how many people would be considered in His broader group of followers—perhaps 70? 200? Maybe more? Jesus' fan club is growing, and many more are looking toward Him as an influencer in Jerusalem. How many of them does Jesus know by name, know well enough to bring their faces and character to the Father for consideration as part of His inner circle? We are not really sure. We are also not sure if Jesus imagined each person face by face, name by name until He arrived at 12, or if He knew that His limit would be 12. We are not enlightened to the exact process. I like to imagine that Jesus dialogued with the Father about each and every person He knew sitting at the bottom of the hill.

That would take all night.

Not to just get through the lists of people, but to wrestle with the implication of each one being in His small, intimate group of 12. How long did it take to consider the character and personality of each as He spoke with the Father? There are so many variables to consider: group dynamics, interpersonal relationships, expectations, and family dynamics. Safe to say that Jesus didn't do "eeny, meeny, miney, mo." As we set out on our journey of Just 12, the most important aspect is prayer.

Think for a second about your network. Not your contacts in your phone or on your social media follower list, but your network of friends and acquaintances. Think of the people with whom you interact with on a regular basis, regular enough to picture faces, perhaps recall names. Think of your family, your circle of friends, your neighbors, your coworkers, maybe even the people you see every time you go to the places you shop or workout or eat...you get the idea. When you start putting that list together, it's not difficult to get overwhelmed with the idea that you should be responsible to make disciples of all of them. But 12, that's doable right? It might not be easy. It will require change and most likely sacrifice. Twelve is a whole lot more attainable than hundreds. It's also a whole lot more challenging than outsourcing disciple-making to the professionals.

But how do we know who our 12 should be?

Start by making a list.

Start writing down names and bring those names to God for consideration. Remember, these are the people you believe that God is calling you to invest in like Jesus invested in His 12. That's something you want God to have your back on, right? Maybe some people have already come to mind. Maybe some of those people are a no-brainer, maybe others need a little bit more discernment.

As you work on your list, consider a few things about your 12 by looking a little closer at Jesus' 12. Because those in Jesus' 12 have a lot to teach us about who we are called to make disciples makers of.

Here are Jesus' words (with some emphasis added) about disciple-making disciples. Jesus said, "All authority in heaven and on earth has been given to me. Therefore go and make disciples *of all nations*, baptizing them in the name of the Father and of the Son and of the Holy Spirit, and teaching them to obey everything I have commanded you. And surely I am with you always, to the very end of the age" (Matthew 28:19-20).

When we put making disciples of all nations next to Jesus' words found in the narrative about the early church, a pattern emerges. (again with some emphasis added)…"But you will receive power when the Holy Spirit comes on you; and you will be my witnesses in *Jerusalem, and in all Judea and Samaria, and to the ends of the earth*" (Acts 1:8).

Jesus gives a clear directive that there are no exclusions but also as to who gets to hear about Him and learn to be a disciple of His. That "all nations" and "ends of the earth" stuff—that's not just about proximity and geography, that's also about race and culture and diversity. Making disciples of all nations and being witnesses to the ends of the earth is about inclusion. Jesus' final directive before departing our existence on Earth was to ensure that there are no exclusions on who gets an invitation to enter His kingdom. We get a glimpse of this even within Jesus' 12. At first appearances the 12 seem pretty plain—a bunch of Jewish men. But there are more than a few surprises when it comes to those Jesus included.

Political Diversity

The political scene in Jesus' day wasn't a two-party system. Multiple competing stories shaped the worldviews, values and politics of the people that Jesus encountered every day. The influences behind these storylines are at work in Jesus' 12, too. Think for a second about the heated debates that could, and perhaps do, erupt at the Thanksgiving table when politics and religion are brought up. Now add to that not just decades but centuries of inculturation. In Jesus' day, there was no separation between religion and politics. The views held were held deeply. At Jesus' table, we find explosive opposing views of how, when, and through whom God was going to do what God had been planning to do for the redemption of the world. But it's not just these worldviews that had potential for conflict.

Money, Money, Money

Perhaps one of the greatest dividers in our culture, and others, is between the haves and the have nots. Jesus' 12 likely consisted of both groups. First, consider Matthew the tax collector. Based on the hate of many Jews towards tax collectors and the story of Zacchaeus, it's pretty safe to assume that this man also known as Levi was in the upper class. He was certainly much better off than the average struggling Isrealite. Peter, Andrew, John and James were likely middle class; even though they could afford the boats and hired hands, they likely saw very little of their efforts turn into substantial wealth because of the high tax rate of both the puppet government and Rome. Although we don't know much about the other disciples, we can assume they were not well to do because of the comments of others. They were dismissed as uneducated and unimportant. They were constantly referred to as "Men of Galilee" or "The Galileans." The tone of such comments is belittling. Galilee was mostly agricultural, which again means most of what was worked for was taken for taxes. They lived paycheck to paycheck, or more accurately, harvest to harvest.

Range in Social Standing

As mentioned, Matthew was a tax collector, and tax collectors were always lumped in with prostitutes and sinners. Tax collectors and sinners appear to be synonymous. The religious elite seemed to have the biggest problem with Jesus' association with tax collectors. On the other end of the spectrum, you had Nathaniel, whom Jesus considered a model Israelite. Throw in some blue-collar fishermen and farmers, as well as the studious Judas, who seems to be a bookkeeper of sorts, and you have quite the range in social status.

Age

We don't know the ages of the disciples. Based on how long many of them lived, we can speculate that most of them were young. We might also want to consider that the life expectancy was not what it is today. Thirty in Jesus' day was middle-aged. Peter, who seems to be a leader of the fishing business, was likely older than many of the others. Perhaps only a few years younger than Jesus. That puts the ages of the disciples between 13 and 30 years of age. Young by today's standards, but diverse for ancient near east standards.

Religious Practices/Spiritual Journey

The above categories have implications that seep into the spiritual maturity and even religious preferences of the disciples. Those who were more influenced by Greek culture may not have attended synagogue and temple regularly, while those who adhered to Jewish law never missed. Discipleship doesn't require that a person go to the same church as you. He or she doesn't need to be a Christian. None of the disciples were Christians when they started; they were all just willing to come alongside Jesus. God will bring people that are willing to come alongside you, so that they can discover more about what it means to be connected to Him through Christ.

The Call of the Everyday and Ordinary

So you may be asking, what's the point?

Let's not exclude people in our 12 because they are rich or poor, because they take a different stance on political issues or have a different social status. The sad reality is that most of our churches today are about as bland as they come. Even churches with some racial mix are culturally and economically narrow. Let's also remember that Jesus brings an interesting mix of experiences. He was the uneducated, illegitimate son of a woman who married a blue-collar worker. He came from a forgettable town on the outskirts of the red light district of a city that housed the retreat home of a puppet king. On the surface, Jesus did not have the pedigree, prestige or privileges associated with someone worth following. Let's not let our prejudices and preferences blind us to how God might want to partner with us in the lives of the people He has connected to us.

From what we understand about Jesus and the times, within this group of men, there were all sorts of labels to be had: nationalists; xenophobics; swindlers and schemers; Bible thumpers and sacrilegious; maybe even hotheads, extremists and passivists; farmboys and hipster urbanites; simpletons and sophisticates. Yet none of those things blacklisted any one of Jesus' 12. At the same time, one of the labels not given to any of Jesus' 12 was "extraordinary." By all measures, these 12 were ordinary, simple, everyday people with no credentials, authority or license that qualified them to be apprenticed and led by Jesus—let alone be responsible for passing on the ways of Jesus to others.

Don't be surprised when someone in your 12 is a person others might exclude. Your 12 will be unique to your context and calling. Don't be surprised that God might bring to mind some people that you might not normally pick. Don't be surprised if someone who struggles with depression, gender identity, substance abuse, sexuality or violence becomes a potential 12 for you. One of your 12 might be an illegal immigrant, a refugee or an undocumented worker. They might be unchurched or just over church. When Scott talks about the 12 in his list, he shares that half of them he wouldn't have picked, if not for prayer. I have someone on my list I honestly wanted to exclude, and it was in a time of prayer that I felt deeply convicted to circle their name instead of dismiss it.

Scott and I can't think of any group or person we could justifiably exclude from those who could end up in our 12. If God breaks our heart for someone, impresses on us to invest, then we listen to God and start living the way Jesus did with His 12. The selection of your 12 is between you and God. There is no Scripture that people can twist and use to dissuade you from your calling. That might bring up a whole lot of questions, such as "what about my kids or my spouse?" We'll address that in the following chapters. For now, just remember that there are no exclusions. As you contemplate your list, remember this is not about people who fit your preferences. Nothing disqualifies anyone from being loved by you like Jesus loved His 12.

Relationally Receptive

There is something that Jesus' 12 did have something in common that is worth highlighting. All of Jesus' 12 were relationally receptive to Him. They were open to His invitation. It's not likely any of us will just walk up to one of our 12 and say, "Come follow me." But as we think through our 12, as God both brings people to mind or brings people into our path, one of the key indicators should be how open and willing they are to engage in a relationship. It's going to be hard to love 12 people like Jesus loved 12 if they are never available. We have to be able to interact at some level to be able to live this model of Jesus. It doesn't make much sense to put your hairstylist as one of your 12 when you see that person only occasionally. If, however, that hair stylist bumps into you at the gym or kids' activity, and you get a nudge to invite them to Sunday brunch and they say yes, God might be leading you to consider them in your 12. Relational receptivity is one of the few qualifiers for your 12. It's not exclusionary to not include someone who never says yes to being included.

4 Deep Wells

When I was thirteen I got to go on my first trip to Canada with my grandparents. My older brother was supposed to go, but he got in trouble (no, not Works Bombs). I have so many memories of that trip, but for some reason I have this image of the bait shop that we would regularly visit for supplies. Typically we used leeches and earthworms. We smuggled the earthworms in from the U.S., though I don't think it was illegal. My grandpa had been raising hundreds of them since they were just wee little things. Random, I know. Anyway, we had to pick up leeches from the bait shop, where there were all kinds of creepy-crawly, slippery-slimy creatures we could choose from: crawfish, leeches, minnows and worms. And they came in a bunch of sizes. They awaited their dreadful fate in a giant, bluish-green deep well. If you've never stepped into a bait shop, just imagine large utility sinks filled two-thirds full with fish. The bait shop worker would reach down and scoop up a net full of leeches. On a few occasions, my grandpa would ask for a couple of crawfish or bigger minnows. My grandpa stuck to what worked, but he also knew that what works doesn't always work. He did catch a pretty big bass with one of those crawfish.

What does this have to do with choosing your 12?

It might be easy to just stick with what you know works. However, in order to fully experience pouring into 12 people like Jesus did, we need to have a little more diversity in our selection. Think about your 12 in these four deep wells.

Family

Friends

3Ls (the lost, lonely and least)

Enemies

Prescriptive methods don't always stick. Yet Scott and I think of these buckets as essential. Essential in that they are represented in our 12, but not necessarily equally. Having people who live in each of these areas brings harmony, growth and impact to our mission. Diversity in our 12 will help challenge our perceptions and perspectives (that are far from objective). Diversity in our 12 enriches our current reality with a glimpse of God's kingdom. His is a kingdom of grand diversity that makes room for all tribes and nations—for children and elders, widows and workmates, and perhaps even an enemy.

Family (Deep Well 1)

If you are married, then your spouse needs to be in your 12. No, the Bible doesn't say this, but your spouse as one of your 12 is intuitive and part of the strategy. And it's Christ-like. The commitment and the vows you make in marriage are no less than a commitment to love like Jesus loved. And if disciple-making is loving our 12 like Jesus loved His 12, then our spouses need to be on our list.

Think for a minute about the implications of looking at marriage as a relationship that is focused on displaying and conveying the love of Christ and helping the other person do the same. Most Christian marriages already make this commitment.

It would be strange not to have your spouse in your 12. Your 12, after all, are the people into whom you are pouring the majority of your energies and efforts. These are the people you are giving your attention to, scheduling your life around, being interruptible for, and putting their interests above your own. It only makes sense that your spouse would be in your 12, right? Not having our spouse in our 12 is a recipe for a neglected and resentful marriage partner. Our 12 take priority over other relationships. They have to because of our limited capacities in our limited world. Married people have made a vow, a covenant agreement to not choose others over their spouse.

To our single friends who have rightly felt that the U.S. church has historically neglected and even ostracized those who are single, please hear this: Not being married doesn't make you less effective at loving others like Jesus did. It does not make you less effective at carrying out His mission and message or using His methods. It is those of us who do have spouses that need to take very seriously, maybe more seriously than ever before, that our partners are the first in our list of 12.

Much of what has just been stated could be stated for children, as well. Parents are not just the primary spiritual influence in their children's lives; they are, for a certain period of time, uniquely positioned for making disciple-makers of their children. Parenthood is one of the primary metaphors used to translate the ideas and methods of discipleship in Jewish culture to the border Greco-Roman world. In his writings, Paul (the missionary) and author of many letters to the early church, rarely if ever specifically mentions discipleship or disciple-making. Rather, he writes and relates to "sons and daughters" who are part of a new family through adoption. These sons and daughters are not just adopted by God, but cared for and coached by trustworthy followers. Parenting is a natural on-ramp for teaching obedience to the ways of Jesus. Our children see and hear the model of faith we put on display for them everyday until they reach adulthood. And even after that, they will continue to look toward us. Pre-adult children are as close to mandated in our 12 as anyone could be.

Mutual Learning

This might be a good time to mention the idea of mutuality in disciple-making relationships. The relationship of our 12 is a reciprocal one. Reciprocal and mutual, meaning that both people in the relationship are learning from each other (whether they know it or not). Similar to the Jewish proverb, "Who is Wise? He who learns from everyone," Paul instructs those who are learners to share with their teachers, saying, "Those who are taught the word should share all good things with their teacher" (Galatians 6:6).

Even Jesus exemplified movement towards mutuality with His 12. Although He is the prototype for a perfect humanity—the teacher, not the student—He moved to a place in His relationships where His students became His friends.[15] Discipleship is not about hierarchy. There is no ladder to climb. There are no colored belts we will wear around our robes in heaven. There is not some ranking system based on outperforming others. There is one Ruler, and the rest of us are followers. The rest of us as followers have something to learn from anyone and everyone on the journey.

Learning from others includes children and students, even those younger than us. It includes those generations ahead of us who might not have as much clarity of mind they once had or adapt to the fast changing technologies and cultures of our current world. Just the other day, my son taught me something about faith. I often learn more from my kids about theology and faith than I have ever learned from classrooms and professors. It was pretty simple (there it is again). I asked him to help me use a shop vac to clean up a project I was working on. And my five-year-old complied without hesitation. He was eager to help even before I told him we would be using the super-cool shop vac. When we were done, I sensed a divine nudge that said, "That's childlike faith. Children desire to be a part of what their parents are up to... until they're nine years old. How often are you, Jake, more eager to have Me join you, rather than you joining Me?" Okay! God taught me something through my son, and that same thing can happen in every relationship. God can use anyone to teach us about Him.

Brother Keepers and Babysitting Parents

A friend recently said, "I feel like I'm parenting my parents. When did this happen?"

Giving thought to having a sibling or parent in your 12 is worth consideration, but doesn't carry the same weight as a spouse or pre-adult child. Jesus' brother wasn't in His 12. Just because you are close to your siblings or cousin, or just because your parents are now empty nesters or are the closest people in your life doesn't mean they will make it into your 12. They might. But we urge caution to defaulting to filling up your 12 with those connections who are the most natural and easiest for you. As stated earlier, don't exclude them, either. If God is nudging you towards a brother or sister, mother or aunt, or even grandfather, take some time to pray it through.

Friends – a Few Good Iron Sharpeners (Deep Well 2)

Proverbs 27:17 tells us *"As iron sharpens iron, so a friend sharpens a friend."*

The poet of an ancient book of Jewish wisdom says a cord of three strands is not easily broken.[16] Jesus seems to be working on building a strong cord within His 12. We see over and over again in the narratives about Jesus that He took Peter, James and John aside. These three are often referred to as "The Three." Within His 12, Jesus set time aside to be with just these three guys. Now, this book isn't called "Just 3" (maybe that's a good future book), but for the sake of understanding our 12, it's important to note how Jesus brought these three into another level of transparency and vulnerability. At the end of His ministry, Jesus calls all of His disciples His friends,[16] but these three have strong ties that look more like a strong cord.

Do you have two to four people in your life that you call your closest friends that can be a part of your 12? These are people who aren't afraid to speak up, people whom you can challenge, as well as be challenged by. These are people with whom you can imagine going on vacation. Think about it for a second. Jesus spent a lot of time with His 12 and even more time with the three. I can't imagine He wanted to take three people up a mountain[17] that He couldn't stand being with on a road trip.

Seeing how learning to love like Jesus is reciprocal, our buckets could include mentors, teachers and parents. These are people who are good at creating safe places for us to share our struggles, challenges, sins, celebrations, and dreams. People whose agenda for us is to grow more and more into the person God designed us to be. Hopefully you already have some names that come to mind. If not, perhaps reserve some space in your 12 for God to bring some your way.

Lost, Lonely and Least (Deep Well 3)

Take a look at a few ways Jesus talks about His purpose and mission.

> "For even the Son of Man came not to be served but to serve, and to give his life as a ransom for many." (Mark 10:45)

> Jesus answered them, "It is not the healthy who need a doctor, but the sick. I have not come to call the righteous, but sinners to repentance." (Luke 5:31-32)

> "The thief comes only to steal and kill and destroy; I have come that they may have life, and have it to the full." (John 10:10)

> "I have come into the world as a light, so that no one who believes in me should stay in darkness." (John 12:46)

Jesus had a mission for the lost, the least and the lonely, for people who are alone and feel the weight of the broken world. People who have felt discarded or dismissed. Those who have felt like life is stacked against them. Jesus loved them all. Those who have made poor choices, and those who have had to live with the consequences of others' poor choices. His mission was about people who have wandered or have been left wondering.

It's interesting how so few of us think of Jesus' 12 in these categories. Why is that? Perhaps it's because conventional disciple-making practices focus on those who are on the inside (whatever "inside" might be). We forget that Jesus' 12 were the outsiders. When Jesus says it's the sinners who need a doctor, not the healthy, that's a response to the religious elite of His day and their reaction to Jesus investing in and including Matthew the tax collector as one of His disciples. It's at Matthew's house, at Matthew's table, that Jesus says this. His 12 were the lost, the lonely and the least. His 12 were lost and found by Him. They were the least, and He elevated them, making Himself their servant. They were alone in an ever-darkening world, and He gave them light.

Our 12 can have space reserved for people whom others might deem irreligious, or even sacrilegious. You know people who have been made to feel like they don't belong within a hundred feet of a church building. Those who have bought into the lie that God has abandoned them, and many more who have been forgotten by the church or made to feel like they are a project in need of fixing. If we do not find space in our 12 for the least of these, then we are not much aligned with Jesus.

What About Judas? (Deep Well 4)

It's pretty popular (and healthy) to eliminate toxic people from our lives. We don't want to advocate sticking around in abusive and manipulative relationships. However, we do see something in Jesus' model of His 12 that is worth noting.

Few people in all of literature are as famous for betrayal as Judas. We see Brutus in Shakespeare's *Julius Caesar*, but he's a distant second. Judas hands Jesus, his teacher and friend, over to those who were hell-bent on His destruction. Hell-bent not just on His death but His humiliation, His utter embarrassment, so that His heresy and waywardness would be put to an end. And it's not just that Judas tipped off the authorities; he led the way. Judas leaned over with a kiss on the check, he looked

Jesus in the eyes...a decision he would regret enough that he'd take his own life.

And yet, even when Jesus knew Judas would betray Him, Jesus still washed his feet. Jesus still broke bread at the table with him. Jesus still passed him the cup. Judas missed it, but Jesus still offered the invitation to be in communion with Him.

We don't know when Jesus knew Judas would betray Him, but Jesus was the best person in history at knowing and understanding the human heart. Time after time, He seems to be able to read the minds and hearts of those plotting against Him, whispering to themselves, mumbling under their breath. It's hard to imagine that Jesus was totally clueless to the poisoned heart of Judas, whether or not He fully knew the extent to which Judas would go or when. And yet, Jesus still loved Judas.

So here is the dreaded question.

Who
is
your
Judas?

It doesn't have to be that person who hurt you more than any other person in the world. Likely it will not be that person. You'll have other work to do with that person. Everyone has people in your life that let you down, that caused you pain, or maybe they just are a pain in general. Your Judas might be that frustrating person at work or that neighbor that likes to gossip. Or maybe that guy at the gym that doesn't respect your personal time and space. Chances are that one or two people have aleady come to mind. Might God be asking you to make them part of your 12? Again, spend some time presenting this person to God, and maybe presenting your case as to why you don't want to do it. Let God do some work on your heart and see what you sense.

Let's go back once more to those toxic relationships. If you are in an abusive or manipulative relationship, think twice about adding that person to your 12. Don't go picking a Judas because you think you are going to save someone who tends to walk all over you. Boundaries are still important and still apply, and one of those boundaries might be to release someone who has been dangerous to your soul, life, mind or heart. It might mean offering that person to God and trusting that His Spirit will lead them into someone else's 12.

But What About...?

Undoubtedly, you have questions. How formal is this commitment? Do you tell the person, or ask permission to include them? What if someone asks if they are in your 12, or if they can be in your 12? What about someone who is the opposite gender? How long are people in your 12? Before we get to the questions, let me offer a little encouragement: don't get hung up on finding your 12 before moving on to the next chapters. At the writing of this line, neither Scott or I have a full dozen people yet. Just 12 is about adopting the small, slow, simple and sustainable model of Jesus. If at this moment you have even just one person you are sure is in your 12, then you can start applying what is presented in the following pages. The rest of your 12 will come. In fact, as you continue to read, you might gain more clarity and insight into your 12.

Now, back to the questions. Two words guide the answers to these questions and more that you might have: context and conviction. Most of the questions above and those you are contemplating likely don't have universal answers. The answers will require some thoughtful reflection on the situations, environments and cultures in which you find yourself. This, alongside the values and beliefs you hold, will help guide you. Answers may change over time as you and your circumstances change. Below are a few thoughts and opinions regarding some common questions.

What about someone who is of a differing gender (that isn't your spouse)? Jesus may not have had women in His 12, but He did create safe spaces where He made significant spiritual and relational investments in women. It can only be speculated as to why no women were in Jesus' 12. Whether for cultural reasons or theological ones, we will leave that debate to others. Because of the wide contexts and convictions of followers of Jesus, we will also not draw any hard and fast lines on this matter. We do suggest that guidelines and boundaries are essential for those who do choose to have someone from the opposite gender in their 12. Those guidelines are about developing mutual trust and respect, versus fear and legalism. One pastor writing on this matter says, "Boundaries between genders should be informed by hospitality rather than legalism." Hospitality, he says, creates spaces that focus on physical and emotional elements that provide safety.[18] Honoring the mental, emotional, physical and spiritual well-being of the other is of utmost importance in all relationships and is especially helpful in discipleship-focused relationships across gender divides. Certainly it is essential for those who are married to discuss with their spouse the potential of discipling somone from a differing gender. For those who are unmarried, seeking the discernment of a trusted and wise friend regarding your choices of the opposite gender would be smart as well. Limits to such a relationship do exist, as some topics are off-limits for discussion and sharing (as you will see in later chapters). This limitation may not mean excluding someone, but it should be taken into account.

Many of the questions above are birthed from this question: how formal is this commitment? This book is written with a bias towards the informal. This is likely unfamiliar and potentially uncomfortable territory for many, especially those who have experienced a more formal process of faith development (overseen by professionals). Given that the majority of readers are living in a post-Christian context, we are advocating for this process to be informal by and large. Some contexts, like college campuses or Christian workplaces, might lend themselves to a more formal commitment where invitations of a discipling relationship might be more easily extended. Likely you will have only a few of your 12 that relate in a more formal commitment. Formalizing a discipling relationship carries the danger of becoming overly focused on process and outcomes. Formalization can also carry the connotation of spiritual hierarchy, of one person being an expert because of how long they have been a Christian or how much religious education they have received. As you will continue to see, we are trying to move away from processes or programs that create complexity or seek to control outcomes.

There is a small chance that your reading of this book and committing to selecting 12 will lead to someone asking if they are or could be in your 12. One of my friends asked if they could be in my 12. They already were. Chances are if someone is that relationally receptive to you that they ask, they probably will be in your 12. But what if you get a real sense that this person isn't one of your 12? Say, for example, if you are at your relational capacity, or you were reserving space from one of the other buckets. Let's remember that Jesus still cared for and loved others outside His 12. One of His closest friends, Lazarus, was not in His 12. If you have to inform someone that they are not in your 12, do it gently and remind them that it doesn't mean you are not in a relationship with them, only that you sense there are others who will require a more intentional investment.

How long do you stick with your 12? Chances are that each of your 12 will be in your 12 for a different period of time. Your spouse is in your 12 until death do you part. Your kids are likely the same, but perhaps there may be a season after they reach adulthood (in their late 30s) where they will not be. It may be a good practice to reevaluate your 12 at least every three years. In that time, changes in proximity and relational receptivity may occur that will indicate it is time to make some changes. Just 12 is not a perfect system; it's a strategy modeled after Jesus.

Context and conviction are a big part of selecting your 12. As you wade through the messiness of having 12 people you are loving like Jesus, you will need these to be your guide. For some, selecting 12 will be the first instance of hearing from God. In a few chapters we will talk about the importance of soul refueling. Practices that grow dependency on God and His Spirit are essential. Connecting with God and experiencing His love is core to faith. For those who are beginners in sensing God's voice/nudge (or whatever you want to call it), here are a few ways to increase your receptivity to how He might be leading.

Pay attention to what seems fortuitous or coincidental. If you have an unplanned encounter with someone on your potential list of 12, someone you have prayed for or asked God to give you insight about, pay attention to how that encounter goes. Look for and listen to cues as to the potential for them joining your 12. Perhaps they are about to move out of town (maybe that means it's a no). If they share something in a more authentic way, ask for help, or invite you to something, it might be an indicator that God is providing an opportunity for greater relational investment. I was about to eliminate someone from my potential 12 when I got a call from them the next day. I didn't think they were relationally receptive. Turns out they were just busy. It also turns out they were looking for some way to come alongside me spiritually.

Pay attention to your body when you pray for or consider a certain person. Do you get anxious or lighthearted, irritated or calm? Someone who makes us anxious probably isn't a person who we think of as an iron-sharpening friend. On the other hand, irritability might be the exact reaction to expect when contemplating your Judas. Weigh the sense you're getting against your common sense.

Pay attention to the words and images that come to mind. As you pray, write down a person's name or picture them in your mind (or both). Where does your mind go from there? If God brings to light a specific need, circumstance or image, take note of it. If something is brought to the forefront of your mind (and there might not be), keep it there over the next few days to see if something aligns. If it does, it might be an indicator to include that person.

Pay attention to Scripture. During your selection process, read through one of the narratives about Jesus, the book of Acts, or one of the letters to the early church. As you read, have your list of potential 12 nearby. If someone on your list suddenly bursts off the pages as you read, make an indication by circling or underlining their name.

The process of selecting your 12 isn't something to get hung up on. Don't let it keep you from moving forward, even if you have only one person you're committed to. As you start to live the final command of Jesus, the practices that help make disciple-makers and who those people might be will become more clear. In this process, you will also be developing your relationship with God through Christ and learning to listen and depend on His Spirit.

Re-Present

As disciple-making disciples, we don't just re-present Jesus to our 12 (and to our world); we also are called to re-present our 12 to God. The selection of your 12 isn't the end of your prayers. Jesus doesn't stop presenting His 12 to the Father. He continually brings His followers and friends, petitioning on their behalf. Even on the night before His death, Jesus' prayers were for His 12. Jesus prays for His 12 until the very end. Helping others follow after Jesus doesn't just begin in prayer, it is completely and utterly dependent upon the work of God's Spirit. Prayer for your 12 is necessary. One of the greatest actions we can take in loving our 12 and helping them live more under the rule of Jesus is to pray for them.

Questions for Reflection and Discussion

1. Who already comes to mind in your selection of 12?

2. Selecting family and friends to be in your 12 probably comes easy to most. How did you feel when it was suggested to include the lost/lonely/least or your enemy?

3. What challenges or opportunities do you see including the 3 Ls?

6

Socialize and
Serve

"Christianity has lost its place
at the center of American life.
Christians must learn how to live
the gospel as a distinct people
who no longer occupy the center
of society. We must learn to build
relational bridges that win
a hearing."

–HUGH HALTER, *THE TANGIBLE KINGDOM:*
CREATING INCARNATIONAL COMMUNITY

CHAPTER 6

DON'T WAIT TILL SUNDAY

So now that you've started on your 12, the rest is easy. All you have to do next is get in touch with them and tell them you are going to start discipling them.

Awkward.

Even more awkward when you next get together.

Jesus' interactions with His 12 didn't appear awkward. Maybe it was a little awkward when Jesus got in Peter's boat and told him how to fish, but the interactions Jesus had as He befriended those who would become His 12 seemed natural and effortless compared to some of our modern packaged forms of discipleship. Perhaps some of the non-awkwardness comes from the universal language spoken through the hospitality Jesus extended to His 12. Invitation and inclusion all but eliminates awkwardness.

We don't have to look at only the narratives of Jesus to see the power of socializing and serving. This book is being written in the middle of the COVID-19 epidemic of 2020. Nearly the entire world is feeling the effects of the social distancing measures put in place to help curb the devastation of the virus. The inability to gather in social settings, to eat at our favorite restaurants, to sing or pray at our places of worship, to send our kids to the neighbors so they are out of our hair for a few moments of sanity, and our inability to socialize is all taking its toll. I have been asking friends that we have finally been able to see face to face, even if only at a safe distance, what they have learned and hope to carry with them from this time. One friend said, "I am going to say yes more. I am not going to make excuses about why I can't go out and be with friends and loved ones." Overwhelmingly, the responses are of a similar vein—something along the lines of going out with friends or having more people over for meals. The consensus centers on greater intentionality with socializing.

Socializing and serving are the ecosystems of relationships. They are like greenhouses for discipleship. They are the essential environments for followers of Jesus to learn and lead a life in His way. What we have experienced in recent history is the overemphasis on classrooms, sanctuaries and stages as the means to reproduce followers of Jesus. As a result, lots of energy and resources have been dumped into strategies that minimize optimal environments for relationships to grow.

There is a word for this kind of relationally focused energy and time. It's not a word you have heard preached on Sunday. It's not a particularly sacred word, but then again, we are in the faith that takes ordinary things and makes them sacred. Scott and I were introduced to this word and its hidden power by a friend of ours, Kim Hammond. It could substitute for the churchy jargon you sometimes hear Christians use. Things like "doing life together" or "doing community together." It's a word that gets lost in the margins and whitespace of the narratives. It's in the whitespace that the world of Jesus' 12 is transformed.

Are you ready for it? The word is . . . *diatribo.*

Well, that's the Greek word for it. It can be found in John 11:54:

> "Therefore Jesus no longer moved about publicly among the people of Judea. Instead he withdrew to a region near the wilderness, to a village called Ephraim, where he stayed with his disciples."

Do you see it?

It's hidden by our modern eyes. Hidden by our ways of seeing things that are so focused on outcomes and measurables. Here it is again. This time untranslated.

> "Therefore Jesus no longer moved about publicly among the people of Judea. Instead he withdrew to a region near the wilderness, to a village called Ephraim, where he DIATRIBO with his disciples."

The way it's used here and in other places in the book of John, as well as in the book of Acts, is referring to the simple act of spending or passing time. Another definition means "to rub together." That's what you and I do when we pass time together. The more we rub shoulders with each other, the more our lives begin to rub off on each other.

Hints of this kind of rich relational environment are all over the narratives about Jesus. Jesus' first miracle was at a wedding celebration, a social event that lasted days, and Jesus' miracle prolonged the celebration. Jesus spends so much time socializing that He was accused of being a drunk and glutton. And the ways in which He socializes, as we mentioned before, bring judgment and challenge from the elites. When Jesus is choosing His 12 and He gets to Matthew (also known as Levi) the tax collector, He ends up having a party at Matthew's house. It's there that Jesus is confronted. That confrontation shows us just how powerful the practice of socializing is. It has the power to include, but also to offend. Jesus gives value to the tax collectors and sinners He eats with, just in the simple act of sitting at their table. This is what prompts the religious leaders to question Jesus' wisdom and authority.

Jesus is constantly and consistently socializing and serving with His 12.

This book was born out of a *diatribo* of socializing and serving. Scott and I have *ditribo(ed)* with coffee and meals, with paint brushes and broomsticks, and even with dodgeballs and Ping Pong balls. Over the years, all that *diatribo* has added up to a whole lot of learning from each other, and a whole lot more vulnerability and authenticity. If we are going to follow Jesus and live out both His faithful example and strategic model, then socializing and serving are going to be a big part of our lives. **We can't do life together if we are not in the places life happens.** In between the stories Jesus tells and the miracles He performs, in the boat trip and road trips, in upper rooms and around tables—these are the places life happens.

What if it's the picnic, parties and potlucks that are the essential part of what it means to be a church? (We are not saying worship, preaching, prayer or reading God's Word are not, but those things don't need to just happen for one hour on a Sunday.) It seems reasonable to conclude that when one of the early church leaders wrote, "Don't stop meeting together as some are in the habit of doing,"[19] they were referring more to parties and potlucks than to programs and productions.

So far, the emphasis has been on socializing. However, socializing and serving go hand in hand, and that's why they are one chapter instead of two. Call it a cycle, instead of a two-step tandem or two rails of the train. Perhaps a good way to think about them is as *synergistic*. They give momentum and power to each other that they could not achieve on their own. One leads to the other, which leads to the other, which leads to the other. It is likely that socializing often comes first when it comes to relationships, but that is not a hard-and-fast rule. Serving can be a form of socializing. Socializing and serving are intertwined and interdependent. It's difficult to serve when you don't know someone well enough to meet a real need. And yet meeting a need can lead to deeper, more intimate relationships. Serving can be a way of socializing where words are not even necessary. Just our presence, with the presence of Christ, carries power that works in the unseen.

Scott grew up on a farm. You wouldn't know it by his city swagger, but he's a born-and-bred hay-slinger from central Illinois. His dad is German and a Marine. In other words, he was never much for words. But one particular act stands out in Scott's mind that moves him to this day. In high school, Scott played baseball. Some of those games took place during the planting season, the time of year that every farmer was out in the fields from the first sign of daylight until after the sun went down. Work consumed the community all day, every day. A sparse scattering of mothers and siblings were in the stands at those games, but in those nearly empty bleachers was also the figure of a man: Scott's dad. Game after game, even as the threats of the wet season approached, he was there.

In those moments, Scott's dad was the embodiment of the self-sacrificial love of God. Sacrificial love displayed in the life, death and new life of Jesus. It's easy to think about serving others through how we give time, talents and resources. But love is not just about what you give; it's about what you give up.

Serving our 12 is not about random or obligatory acts of kindness. Serving is about looking and listening for what God might be up to in someone's life and partnering with God appropriately. Serving is about attitude and action. Our attitude is not something we can fake, at least not for very long. This is the attitude of Jesus described in the early church.

> "Do nothing out of selfish ambition or vain conceit. Rather, in humility value others above yourselves, not looking to your own interests but each of you to the interests of the others. In your relationships with one another, have the same mindset as Christ Jesus."

> "Who, being in very nature God, did not consider equality with God something to be used to his own advantage; rather, he made himself nothing by taking the very nature of a servant, being made in human likeness. And being found in appearance as a man,

he humbled himself by becoming obedient to death—

even death on a cross!" (Philippians 2:3-11)

Our attitude should be the same as Jesus, who gave up His status and power. He emptied Himself to become a servant. Serving isn't just about doing nice things—it's about putting the interest of others above our own. It's about not seeing ourselves more highly than our 12. It's about tearing down whatever false, perceived or man-instituted hierarchy we have put in place. For Scott's dad, it was having to work twice as hard the next few days. For some of us, it might mean a sleepless night with a colicky baby so our spouse can get some rest, or a lawn that goes uncut for an extra day so you can help someone move. It might mean a vacation that gets canceled or a purchase that gets delayed. It might mean saying no to that golf invite or ladies night out because we know our spouse feels overwhelmed or overworked. The list can go on and on.

This kind of mindset means that we are not serving in hopes of a mutual exchange. There is no expectation that we will get anything in return, not even a thank you. It means that, in these relationships (and hopefully many more), we are not keeping score; and we don't have an agenda. It does not mean there are no boundaries, that you're a doormat, or that your whole life is dictated by the needs of your 12. We still need to maintain physical, relational, mental and spiritual health. That's why there needs to be an emphasis on times of solitude and silence, reflecting on Scripture and listening to Christ's Spirit. We'll come back to how this kind of silence and solitude is needed to care well for our souls as we seek to care well for others. The servant mindset of Christ is one that seeks to elevate, not just do kind things.

It's not just what Jesus did to serve His 12. He also served His 12 in what He did not do. The idea that we can serve through what we don't do feels slightly counterintuitive. Yet, this can be true in many ways. To illustrate this concept, think about generosity.

Many people think of generosity in terms of how much money a person gives. If someone gives a million dollars to some important cause, they are seen as generous. Large amounts of money being transferred from one person to another, or to a cause or foundation, makes headlines. But generosity is measured not only by what one gives, but also by what one chooses not to take. In our achievement- and outcome-oriented culture, we hardly notice the generosity of those who have chosen not to take that which is right in front of them. A boss who forgoes a pay raise so more people can stay employed, a kid who holds back at the parade when candy is thrown in front of him so that the children around him can get some too, or even the parent who delays personal aspirations because of the pressing need for a paycheck. We are quick to celebrate those who make extravagant monetary donations, but rarely notice those who make extravagant sacrifice. Many people are extremely generous not because of what they gave, but because of what they didn't take.

Jesus doesn't just serve His 12 in what He does; He serves them in what He doesn't do as well. This comes to mind in two areas: power and speech.

Jesus' 12 didn't just look at Him as a really smart guy with lots of wisdom and some good tips for a better life. They looked at Him as the very author of life, as the one who would redeem and restore the whole world. They used the word *Messiah*. Some often say *Savior*; I like to say *Rescuer*. Regardless, Jesus was more than a profound teacher, and because of that, He had tremendous stature, reputation and respect with His 12. His 12 saw Him as the Son of God. And yet . . .

On the night before He was betrayed, in the upper room above a local man's house, Jesus did the unthinkable. He embodied the message He had been trying hard to impress on His followers—the message of servanthood. A message not just of action but of status and posture. What Jesus *didn't* take was the position of power. He didn't take the position of judgment, control or force. Instead, He humbles Himself to the lowest position. On the night of the Last Supper, that position was the foot washer. Jesus washing dirty feet wasn't about dirty feet. Dirty feet are never just dirty feet. For Jesus, this was about not taking what He could have, so that He could give something only He could give. Peter objected to Jesus' gesture, not just because of the act itself but because of what the act meant. What Jesus was doing was undignified. It should have been beneath Him. Foot washers were the lowest of low positions. So many of Jesus' stories pointed to this very thing, and yet the disciples missed it time and time again. Serving is not just about an act; it is about position and status. The only thing beneath Jesus was the idea that any act of service would be beneath Him.

Serving isn't just about doing something for someone that they cannot do on their own; it's also about not doing something so that others can be elevated to a place they didn't think they deserved. Serving is not taking a position of power, even when it's due to you, or expected, or has always been. It's surrendering privilege and advantage for the sake of others being elevated to the place we or others think we deserve.

Practically speaking, this is difficult to navigate with our 12. We are not likely to show up for a Sunday BBQ with a pitcher of water, a basin and a towel, ready to do a foot washing. It wouldn't have the same meaning and certainly would not have the same impact. So we must diligently look and listen to how the Spirit of Christ is leading us to serve practically as well as spiritually. We look and listen for ways to express the love of God that elevates the value and worth of our 12 to the level that Jesus had for His 12. To lay down our lives for the sake of our 12.[20]

A little bit easier to live out in practical, everyday ways is the second area we see Jesus not doing something. In all the words we study about Jesus, we rarely take the time to study the words He didn't say.

Perhaps you have heard this biblical wisdom before?

> "The tongue has the power of life and death" (Proverbs 18:21).

No one needs to take a poll to know that the words others have said have both launched careers and ended dreams. It's interesting to hear even some of our greatest celebrities and heroes recall how words from someone they looked to for inspiration all but squelched their potential. We have a word for when someone constantly speaks negatively and disparagingly about people and situations: toxic. If you do a quick study on toxic personalities, you will have no shortage of advice about how to avoid them. In some cases, you may even come to realize that you are the toxic one...ouch! You know what you won't find in those searches? Any tie between Jesus and toxic personalities, because Jesus was the opposite of toxic.

George D. Everly, PhD and professor at John Hopkins University, coined a word that gets close to the kind of person Jesus was: he speaks of having a *NUTRIC* personality. It's an acronym:

Nurturing | Understanding | Trustworthy | Reliable | Inspiring | Confident

If you can't remember the whole acronym, a *nutric* personality is a person who supports and nurtures another's growth and development.[21] Is that not part of what Jesus' mission was all about? The growth and development of humanity toward a restored and full life as God desired and dreamed it to be? Granted, the full maturity and restoration of all things takes more than just a *nutric* personality; Jesus' work in His flesh, death and resurrection overcomes all that stands against our ability to live unselfishly and in the right relationship with God and others. And yet, in His interaction with His 12, we see a way of serving that is encompassed by something more than deliverance from the human condition of decay and death.

Can you even imagine Jesus speaking in a way that was disparaging or degrading towards one of His 12? You would be hard-pressed to find anything in the biblical narratives that would lead you to believe anything close to that. When Jesus was with just a few of His disciples, He never had to change the subject when one of the other 12 suddenly walked in. He was never caught talking negatively about any one of His followers. Because He never talked negatively about one of His disciples.

This doesn't mean there wasn't challenge and rebuke, sometimes privately and sometimes with others in earshot. It's likely hard for us to hear words of rebuke and challenge and think they don't carry some sort of negative or disparaging tone. Typically the rebukes we give and receive are tainted with a tinge of jealousy, envy, pride, inconvenience, impatience—or a litany of other self-enhancing, self-preserving or self-serving agendas. But with Jesus, His words of challenge were for the benefit and betterment of the listener.

Jesus served His 12 by never berating, belittling, exasperating, embarrassing or disparaging them.

This way of serving is a great gift from Jesus to His 12 and a great gift we can give to ours. It makes us safe and life-giving people. We fulfill one of those purposes of Jesus, to give life to the full, when we withhold speaking negatively about our 12. This will be especially powerful if we follow the guidance for who we have in our 12. If in our 12, we have those with whom we disagree or struggle to understand or empathize, this way of serving will communicate value and worth. It will speak powerfully to our spouse and children. It will transcend the division that exists between those who are different from us. It will strengthen the ties of close friendship and bridge the gap that exists with our enemies. Speaking life into our 12 isn't just about saying kind and meaningful words; it's also holding back the defeating power of speaking death.

A final thought. Many discipleship strategies are much more regimented than what we are suggesting. There is a time and place for more regimented and programed forms of discipleship—forms that take on the role of mentor or apprentice relationship. Socialize and serve practices don't negate that work; they strengthen and validate it. If that's your preferred way, you don't need to stop; just add some other ways of interacting to your strategy.

Remember . . .

A meal is never just a meal.

Dirty feet are never just dirty feet.

So much of Jesus' ministry happens around socializing and serving. And those ways of befriending, healing, challenging, encouraging and more come from a desire to make known the heart and vision of God. Those things have the power to open up space to share stories, to share our reality.

Questions for Reflection and Discussion

1. How have you been served by others?
2. How have you seen Proverbs 18:21 (pg 98) play out in your life?
3. If you have already identified possible people in your 12, what are some ways to socialize and serve them?

7

Share Your Reality

"There is a beautiful transparency
to honest disciples who never
wear a false face and do not
pretend to be anything but who
they are."

– BRENNAN MANNING,
RAGAMUFFIN GOSPEL

CHAPTER 7

SPEAKING OF JESUS

We've got a friend we'll call Rick, because that's his name. Rick will talk about Jesus no matter the place, the situation, the conversation. Rick once told me about how he was sharing his faith in the hardware store, standing in the lumber aisle. "We were talking about projects and our hometown, and then I just said 'Speaking of Jesus...'" I stopped him and asked, "Wait, did he say something about Jesus?" Rick looked at me, puzzled. "No. Does it matter? Isn't everything about Jesus?" My favorite thing about Rick is that he would do stuff like this all the time. Rick will talk about Jesus even when the opportunity is far from a natural part of the conversation. Rick is a rare breed of Jesus-follower that is gifted with a mix of courage and charisma. Alongside his story of faith, his way of sharing is powerful and effective. Maybe you know someone like this. We have another friend, JR, who can turn from baseball to Jesus in a microsecond. It's this gift, commonly referred to as evangelism, that also presents a bigger set of challenges for many everyday followers of Jesus. For many of us, if we do what Rick and

JR do, it comes across as unnatural and disingenuous, and it's rarely effective. The results leave many of us feeling like talking about faith is reserved only for those with this unique gift.

The Problem with Sharing Our Faith

However is termed—"sharing our faith," "being a witness," or "giving our testimony,"—talking about what we believe is intimidating. This is especially true as talking about Christian faith has become more taboo in our culture. In recent years, typical Christians in America have moved away from feeling a responsibility for personal action when it comes to making Jesus and His mission known. This mentality only adds to the brutal reality of the declining Christian influence in our country.[22] Perhaps some of the apprehension of those who desire to share their faith, and those who might be receptive, is that speaking of Jesus has been so regulated.

The church throughout history seems to pendulate between two extremes. To one side is the swing toward a zealous commitment to faith-sharing. We see "come-to-Jesus" concerts and revivals, courses for debating and defending Christian ideas and doctrines, and equations with diagrams that simplify faith to a transaction of four steps that will determine a person's eternal existence. On the other side is the swing toward a privatization of faith, or a personalized faith that doesn't need to be need to be discussed. It's a faith that is displayed in moral and ethical behaviors and sometimes includes invitations to religious functions. It's a faith that gets displayed on bumper stickers and T-shirts, or in fumbled paraphrases of our favorite podcast or YouTube preacher. Speaking about Jesus has become something other than speaking about Jesus, or when Jesus is spoken about, it is in controlled spaces or prescribed approaches.

This quote is attributed to St. Francis of Assisi: "Preach the Gospel at all times. If necessary, use words." A quick study of St. Francis and the evolution of the misquote reveals that "if" replaced "when." *When necessary, use words.* We are people of words—words are necessary. And, our words and actions need alignment. Sharing our faith includes both the telling and the showing, the saying and displaying. Our words must align with our ways. The methods and the message need to match. When they don't, we come off as judgmental or hypocritical, which apparently is exactly how Christians have been coming off. The fear of being judgmental and coming across as hypocritical adds to our apprehensiveness about sharing.

Think for a moment of the places where you have shared your faith, the times where speaking of Jesus is permitted or welcomed, or when you worked up enough courage to respond to a Spirit-filled boldness. Perhaps it was at a church function, in a group or team where you were asked to give your testimony. Chances are you gave something of a history of your life and faith tradition. When our faith-sharing opportunities have been limited to Bible camps and small groups, we tend to ramble on about the whole story of our lives, unsure which parts are important and awkwardly fumbling through some of the more religious experiences and events. Or perhaps you are one of those few people, like the Apostle Paul, that have a Damascus Road experience,[23] and so you shared about your conversion experience. Or maybe you prayed for an "opportunity" at Thanksgiving, and what started as an empowered conviction was soon perceived as some sort of political or ethical rant, so you were relieved when someone changed the subject to something less awkward and serious. Maybe you've gone to a training or class and had to go put what you learned into practice. Then after going door to door or encountering a stranger on the street, you went through the steps where you presented the diagram, or you told the rehearsed story. Yet when it was all said and done, even in those instances that were well received, maybe even producing the outcomes you hoped for, you were left feeling like something was not natural, not quite authentic and real.

And so the pendulum swings, from attempts at inducing conversions of faith to posing and projecting the faith. In the midst of the back and forth, many followers of Jesus default to a faith that is more religious than relational. We fluctuate between feeling like we are not saying enough or not saying the right things, and feeling like we are not living "good enough." It's no wonder that in this climate of "faith-sharing" we have found ourselves settling for the occasional invitations to church-related activities and social media posts, featuring inspirational Scripture plopped onto a serene nature scene.

The sharing of a tangible journey of the everyday, ordinary follower of Jesus has all but been left out of most people's idea of following Jesus. What is needed for our 12 is not a faith-sharing that turns conversations into transactions, nor one that is about getting our moral and ethical act together and putting it on display. What is needed is a shift from a sharing only at religious venues or when someone asks, to a sharing that overflows from casual conversation. A shift from telling our whole life story, or the story of a spectacular experience, to one that shares how the divine can be found in every moment. It's a sharing that shifts to what is happening in the present, as well as the past. It's a shift from people as projects, in need of conversion, towards people as friends who we let in on our journey toward obedience in Christ. It's sharing the many stories that make up a bigger story of God's continuous pursuit of us. This is a shift toward an authentic and vulnerable sharing of our reality.

A Case for Authenticity

"The kingdom of God is near."

This was the announcement of Jesus when He started His earthly ministry. This was the good news that Jesus proclaimed. This was Jesus' gospel.

For the vast majority of Jesus' listeners, this was not what they were experiencing. God's kingdom felt far away to anyone within earshot of Jesus' words. Not because it wasn't real, but because they were looking at the world through a different lens. It was a lens of self-preservation. Generation upon generation reached and clamoured for power, wealth and influence through the pathways of the world: violence, war, allegiances, oppression, assimilation...The list continues and vacillates as the nation of Israel tries to find life outside the Life-giver and Sustainer. As Jesus spoke the words about the Kingdom of God intersecting with the world of men, it rang in the ears of people who were as desperate for it as they were doubtful it would ever come.

Jesus showed up and revealed how things really are. God in flesh brought with Him the reality of who God is and how the Kingdom works, and by default, how all creation really works. And it's not like what had ever been visible before. Until the revelation that is Jesus, it had all been shadows, archetypes, hints and signposts. Jesus showed up and uncovered and unveiled what was hidden, invisible and mysterious. What was previously not understood was now made known through Jesus. Through Jesus, God is being authentic and vulnerable. He is displaying His nature, character, purposes and will in a profoundly revealing way. It is only through God being authentic and vulnerable that reality is made known. This is why the biggest obstacle in faith-sharing is not a lack of knowledge, maturity or training—it's the desire to protect, hide, cover and withhold.

Firsts and lasts are often memorable. I can remember almost every message I have preached for the first and last time at each church where I have served. I don't think I could give the whole message verbatim, or even the CliffsNotes version, but I remember lots of other details. I remember what I felt like, what I was thinking and feeling. I can remember how the room was set up. I can even remember some of the faces in the crowd. For many of those messages, I can also remember conversations I had before and after. My first time preaching at my last church was memorable for many reasons. I remember how you could hear a pin drop when I was telling a story about my birth mother. The dramatic pause was perhaps a little too much. For some, the extent of my authenticity and vulnerability during that sermon was also a little too much. Afterward, I had one person ask if I was from the west coast. She was shocked that I was not, because "no one from the midwest was that authentic and vulnerable." She was not complaining or criticizing; she was grateful as she shared with tears in her eyes about her own estrangement from her daughter because of her substance abuse and her ongoing journey of healing. It was encouraging. More encouraging than the lack of conversation from nearly everyone else. It appeared, and later was confirmed, that my "openness" might not be received so warmly by everyone. Nonetheless, it didn't stop me. I certainly tend to be more comfortable than most about sharing my inner work and struggles. However, it is the belief that Jesus modeled letting others into His reality, especially those He was responsible to lead, that drives my openness.

Jesus shared the reality of His identity, mission, struggles, thoughts and emotions. He shared the reality of God's kingdom and the human condition. His sharing is part of the reason Jesus can call His 12 His friends. Jesus shared His reality in a way that helped His disciples learn what it meant to bring everything under the rule and rescue of God. He shared the reality of the kingdom, His place in it, and the partnership God was and is offering through His very existence. Certainly sharing our reality is more intimidating than conventional means of faith-sharing, but it can also be more powerful.

What Sharing Our Reality Does

Sharing our reality is about more than sharing what many would call our "testimony." That form of sharing is important and has its time and place. What we are encouraging is an ongoing and continuous sharing of the realties you have faced and are facing. It's not just one moment, but rather letting our 12 in on the many seen, and sometimes unseen, moments where God is at work.

When sharing our faith is reduced to a "once upon a time" moment, it is in danger of becoming distant and disconnected from everyday life. Faith connected to everyday life is what our 12 desire to hear, know and embrace. People want to know that what happened two years, 20 years or 2,000 years ago still happens today. People want a "now" liberation, not just a yesterday one. We all want to know that following Jesus is not something detached from our daily existence, but is intricately and intimately a part of our waking and sleeping, our comings and goings. Those of us who have had a significant spiritual milestone event should be grateful, and that event should be told. But it isn't the only thing that should be told. Sharing our reality is about how milestone moments and the dozens or hundreds of other moments where God showed up, or didn't show up, is shaping us more and more into the image of Jesus. Sharing our reality is about understanding and experiencing how God is at work in our world. Sharing our reality is about how being a follower of Jesus has meaning in our unique cultural contexts and personal constructs.

When we share our realities, we give our 12 a window into the raw world of following after Jesus. Our reality rarely has a storybook ending. Jesus' reality isn't all cupcakes and rainbows. (Actually there were no cupcakes and rainbows that we know of.) If socializing and serving are like a greenhouse, an optimal environment for growth, think of sharing your reality as fertilizer. It's the catalyst that cultivates rich and fertile ground for a full life of faith to thrive. Fertilizer, although a mixture of really good stuff, is also a product of the messy, stinky stuff.

Just like Jesus' 12, our 12 are going to be curious as to how our faith works. Faith is something that gets worked out continuously.[24] The working out of our faith means testing the words we think we are sensing from God's Spirit[25] and keeping a close eye on how our thinking about God is affecting our practices of following Him.[26] We learn to do the work of speaking good news of Jesus as Lord[27] and, in doing so, discover the false idols and ideologies we have built up (often unknowingly). Sharing our reality not only helps us work out our faith, it also gives others that freedom and permission to do so as well.

Sharing our reality also produces natural accountability to our stories. It makes authenticity and vulnerability the working mechanism for relationships rather than a policing transaction of keeping spiritual tabs. Having an "accountability partner," in and of itself, does not produce genuine relationships. And perhaps that is why so many

Christians have avoided and struggled to maintain such relationships.

Most of all, or perhaps most pointedly for the purposes of this book, sharing your reality opens up space for others to do the same. Storytelling begets storytelling, honesty begets honesty, and reality unveils reality. The sharing of our realities will help others feel less alone. Sharing our reality is the bridge by which people will connect to our life. We begin to realize in our reality-sharing that we are much more alike than we ever knew. Reality-sharing normalizes others' reality. The mantra of mutual reality telling will become, "Wait, you too?" Where there is not a fortuitous congruency in realities, a new space will open up for compassion and empathy. When reality is authentically and vulnerably shared, we suddenly become involved in the mess of each other's lives. When reality-sharing becomes the practice of our relationships, we get to become a part of each other's complex and beautiful, disturbing and amazing realities.

The ABCs of Sharing Your Reality

So in the spirit of authenticity and vulnerability, do you tell your 12 everything you are thinking and feeling? Everything that happens? We wouldn't suggest it. Here are three ways we can share our reality that points our 12 to Jesus, helps our 12 grow in obedience, and strengthens our own faith. We call them the ABCs—not because they are elementary, but because we hope you remember them.

A: Abiding
B: Blunders
Cs: Challenges and Celebrations

Each of these reallites is tied to how Jesus shares, but is translated to our reality—the reality that none of us is perfect and that we are each on the journey of learning from Jesus and doing what He says.

A: Abiding

What if one of the biggest components of making disciples in the same way Jesus did is not so much about others imitating our best efforts of living a good life, but about sharing with our 12 our practices of surrender and dependency? We refer to these practices as abiding. Disciple-making then is inviting our 12 into this abiding relationship we are building with God.

Jesus spoke of this intimacy, and it's something that poured over into His authority, power and compassion. Naturally, Jesus' 12 wanted to know how Jesus had such an intimate relationship with the Father. So, they asked Jesus how to pray. This seems like a silly question for 12 Jewish-raised men to ask. They knew how to pray. They knew lots of prayers passed down to them over generations. They prayed a prayer called the Shema, which they recited multiple times a day. Something was missing, though. Jesus had something they didn't. Jesus' response is what we now call the Lord's Prayer. The Lord's Prayer has been a template for prayer for many of His followers, but it's more than that; it's also a window into Jesus' reality.

Our Father in heaven, hallowed be your name; your kingdom come; your will be done; on earth as it is in heaven. Give us this day our daily bread. And forgive us our debts, as we forgive our debtors and lead us not into temptation; but deliver us from evil. For thine is the kingdom, the power, and the glory, for ever and ever. Amen.

In sharing this prayer, Jesus unveils the kingdom and its ruler. He shares about the relationship we can have with God, our Father, as His children. He shares God's mission—His kingdom colliding with our plane of existence. He shares needs—daily bread. He shares about relational struggles—forgiveness. He shares the challenges we will face—temptations of evil. And He shares the ultimate submissive reality of who is really in charge of it all when he says of the Father, "Yours is the power and glory...forever."

Sharing our reality through sharing our abiding in Christ is about sharing our prayers, sharing the reality of how we see the world, how we process life, what we hope for, what we stand for and what we depend on God for. Sharing our abiding doesn't have to be as intimidating as it sounds. We don't need to come up with a new Lord's Prayer, but it's also likely that our *abiding* looks and sounds a little different from Jesus and likely different from each other. Practically speaking, you can share:

- How you pray
- What you pray
- As you pray

How You Pray

Sharing how you pray is about the form and function of your prayer times. Maybe you abide through journaling, or maybe you do nature walks and listen to music. Maybe you pray while you run or reflect on Scripture while you drive. Sharing your reality is about sharing how you do your times of abiding. Sharing doesn't have to be super structured. It does need to be the real, authentic and vulnerable you. Letting anyone into your times of abiding is a vulnerable act. This is your intimate time with the creator of the universe, the one who invites you to be closer to Him than any other.

A little side note for those that don't feel like they are all that consistent at abiding: It's okay—you can share that too. *Please* share that. Far too many people think that the only way to connect with God is in some uber-spiritual, crazy early in the morning, hours at a time, every day way...or it doesn't count. We all want to stay connected to Christ. We all want to rest in Him more regularly, to trust in Him more readily, and rely on Him more steadily (day by day by day). Sharing our reality of our inconsistency is as important and maybe as powerful as sharing those times where we get lost in moments of connecting with God. Inconsistency reveals our desperation to be close to God again, and it shows that we are all on the journey of learning to *abide*.

What You Pray

Sharing what you pray is about the content of your *abiding*. What is it that you pray about when you pray? Share with your 12 some of the questions and concerns you bring before God. Talk about how you wrestle through things you don't understand or wish someone else would understand. This overlaps a little to the challenges and celebrations, but there is more here, too. The prayers of Jesus that we have from Scripture cover so much ground, from hopes and dreams for the disciples, to His gratefulness for God's provision, to His struggle with what He sensed God was calling Him to do.

When you share the content of your prayers, you don't have to say, "in my prayer time" or "when I was praying." You can also say things like, "I was asking God" or "I was reflecting about." If you record or write your prayers, you can share those too. It's one of the reasons I like to journal. Not only can I come back to what I experienced in my times of abiding, but I can also share those times with my 12.

Recently I was journaling at a local coffee shop as my kids were doing homework, a tradition I was trying to establish on Thursdays after school with just me and the two oldest. I had just started reading through the book of Matthew, reflecting and then writing some thoughts and questions after each chapter. When I finished writing and closed my journal, my daughter asked me what I was doing. Instead of saying, "Oh, just writing my thoughts," I slid the journal her way and offered, "Here, you can read what I was doing." It was a profound and powerful moment for me. Intimate too. I had no intention at the moment for her to read what I wrote, but there was also nothing I was writing that I wouldn't want her to know. Actually, I'll share it with you, too.

The family tree of Jesus alone points to the patience by which God brings about His kingdom. From generation to generation, time passes, and for some there is obedience and from others, drifting. But God is still at work, always. Moving toward His eternal purposes. He works through dysfunction, through outsiders, through exile. He works in the unexpected, the neglected, the outcast. There is little doubt that God is at work behind the scenes. I trust this is true even in my own life. God, You are always up to something, something good. I don't always see it or understand, but I trust that You are. From the very start of Jesus' story, we are invited into God working in ways that are unlike our own. God, show me Your ways so that I may walk in them.

Now, you don't have to share your journal with your 12, but maybe you will. Maybe you will take a picture of what you wrote, or something you read, and send it off to one of your 12. Maybe you will text a prayer that you prayed, or leave it as a message on a voicemail. Remember, sharing with your 12 is a way to share the reality of how you are processing life and faith, talk about the reality of a Scripture you encountered that was difficult to understand, or an inclination that you are working through. Let's be vulnerable and authentic about the content of our prayer time, about what it is we think, and say and hope while we are connecting with God.

As You Pray
Sharing your abiding is also about inviting your 12 into the times of your abiding. This may not be for every one of your 12, but perhaps like Jesus, you may find there are a few in your 12 that are ready to join you in your times of encountering God. Again, depending on how you do your abiding, this will look different for everyone. It might mean doing a weekly prayer time together, or taking opportunities to pray together on the phone or over video chats. Sharing my reality in real-time prayer has had far-reaching effects with the relational depth I have with many of my 12. Some times of prayer have led to emotional and spiritual healing that would have otherwise been missed, and these times have led to even greater authenticity and vulnerability.

Jesus modeled sharing His reality this way as well. We see Jesus bring His 12 to the garden to join Him as He abides. It's such a familiar place that when Judas betrays Jesus, he knows exactly where Jesus will be. On this occasion, it's late, and the disciples are unaware of the gravity of the situation, thus they fall asleep. This shows us that our 12 may not be at the same place as us. Who knows—we might discover we're not at the same place as them. I have had several occasions when I have invited others into my abiding and have been surprised with the depth and insight they've shown, even those new to following Jesus.

B: Blunders

Jesus didn't have any blunders, but He shared about the propensity and power of all of us to live out of our self-centeredness and self-reliance. We are encouraged by Paul to confess our sins to one another for healing.[28] I like to say "confess your realities," because sin is a major presence in our reality. We live in a sin-sick world, and that sickness has permeated every part of life. Sin is sneaky. Think of blunders as anything that makes you want to hide: that temptation to tell a little lie, to leave out a certain detail, to cover our tracks, or to go silent. These are sure signs of blunders.

It's a good practice to share our mess-ups and mishaps, even the small ones—the times we indulged a little too much at the holiday party, how we let our eyes or mind linger on that cute coworker, or how we felt a tinge of something awfully close to envy when our childhood friend got that new job and now seems to be able to afford the house and car we only dream about.

These confessions become a handhold for our faith and loosen the foothold that hiding has on us. Rather than getting tripped up, we get a hand up out of the hole that our blunder helped us fall into. Sharing these realities, of how there are sins and remnants of sins that we are asking Jesus to help us with, builds trust with our 12. It makes us real people and not self-righteous, religious types who only point out the faults in others.

We have a close friend that recently went through rehab. His prescribed medication for anxiety and depression, alongside self-medication through pounding a few beers to fall asleep or take the edge off, eventually led to a spinout. Rather than hide this blunder, he told everyone in his contact list who he thought needed to hear it from him rather than through the rumor mill. Over that first week of rehab, he sent out dozens of text messages and phone calls, sharing the reality of his circumstances and what led up to them. His sharing led not just to an outpouring of support and encouragement, it led to a deepening of friendships and trust. Confessing this reality led to healing for him well beyond the consequences of overdoing the alcohol and meds.

Leadership, even leadership in the church, has the propensity to avoid sharing blunders. The results have been catastrophic, not just for many of those leaders, but for the people and organizations they lead. This happens when we brush over our mistakes or create an environment that is overly optimistic and leaves no space for mistakes.

Sharing our blunders isn't about the nitty gritty details. **Share from a place of depth, not a place of details.** Details can easily turn into gossip or a distraction. We do not need to give more power to sin than it already has. And we also don't need to give impulses and thoughts that could potentially trip up our 12 and cause them to fall into similar snares as us. When sharing your blunders, go deeper with the authenticity and vulnerability, not deeper with the details.

Sharing our reality in this way can go a step further. Blunder-sharing is a gateway to identity-sharing. Repeated blunders (our own and others') leave many of us with shame. Shame makes us want to hide and cover up. And that hiding often leads us to stay stuck in a cycle of missteps and mistakes. Being open about shame and the wounds left by repeated and willful sin gives our 12 (at least those we know are trustworthy with such information) a peek at the ruts worn into our identity. These ruts are not who we are meant to be or who God is helping us become. Sharing the shame-rutted blunders releases us of the false identity in which we have been entrenched and puts us on a new and solid path. Confessing our shame takes away its power, because shame thrives in the shadows. Healing is made possible only when the light shines into the darkness. Going to the depth of shame in sharing our blunders also gives others an opportunity to speak encouragement and truth that centers and strengthens our identity in Christ.

We can't stress enough the practice of sharing blunders. It will be risky, it will take courage, and it will be worth it. We have found that the vulnerable and authentic sharing of our blunders has not just brought us closer to our 12, but it has also brought us closer to Jesus.

Challenges and Celebrations

That close friend of ours that we mentioned above is always telling me you can't really be friends with someone if you don't know their biggest struggle and greatest joy. Just as Jesus moved toward friendship with His 12, we are moving toward a deep and lasting friendship with our 12.

Challenges are different from blunders, in that they are not necessarily about faults and failures but are more about the struggle of keeping faith and trust in the face of adversity or crises. Think of Jesus in the garden, when He asked God if He might remove the cup—the looming pain and torture that was coming His way. Most of us will never face that kind of challenge, but we do face challenges that require us to persevere, sometimes beyond what we think we can handle. And some of us will face challenges that we cannot handle alone. Sharing our challenges and struggles opens up space with our 12 to build each other up, to encourage and lovingly rebuke each other.

There might be challenges with how to navigate a situation in our family or at work, or there might be a struggle with vocation or calling. It might be a challenge with a decision about where to move or what job to take. Talking to our 12 about the circumstances we face brings our faith to life. Sometimes our challenges include the cancer diagnosis of loved ones, or the crying baby that hasn't let you sleep in months. Be careful not to minimize real struggles. A crying baby that hasn't let you sleep in months can be devastating in its own ways. Don't let the enormity or simplicity of other people's challenges divert you from sharing yours. Sharing the reality of your challenges gives your 12 the information they need to pray specifically for you. Remember, their prayers for you are a big part of their development as followers of Jesus. We are also letting our 12 in on how we are processing and navigating our lives in light of following Jesus. This is the place where we display how we are growing in living under His rule and rescue.

Challenges are not just about the circumstances we find ourselves in. They are also about the inner world we are experiencing because of those external circumstances. Our reality is as much about our feelings and emotions as it is about the context in which we find ourselves. This is not something we need to shy away from. Jesus experienced the fullness of human emotions. He knows what it's like to have flesh and blood and a mind, body and spirit. He shared tears[29] and fears with His 12. He displayed His anger and His joy with His 12. His 12 were privy to His disappointment[30] and disgust.[31] When we look at how Jesus loved His 12, it included Him sharing the ups and downs of His emotions.

Far too many of us can talk about circumstances and leave out how we are feeling. Feelings determine the meaning of our stories and reality. Without expressing our emotions, people can only imagine what we are feeling based on what they would be feeling. That's not sharing our reality, at least not the fullness of it.

In my own experience, it has been the lack of sharing the reality of grief and anger that has caused me to go all sorts of sideways. Feelings are not something to only be managed and processed. They are the inner world behind the outer one, and it's a world we need to let others into. We cannot empathize if we do not begin to understand others' feelings. Neither will others be able to empathize with us if they are unaware of what we are really experiencing. We must reject the lie that feelings are weak and can't be trusted. Feelings alone are not what we put trust in, but feelings are powerful indicators given to us by God to help us learn to navigate the complexities of our reality.

Where's the Party?

Practically speaking, sharing our challenges and celebrations means we invite and include our 12 into our lives in ways that allow them to experience our reality with us. We invite them to the mess when there is a mess, and the party when there is a party. Remember to talk with your 12 about the joys you are experiencing in life. Let them in on the small things that make you smile. This isn't about bragging about your kids, your net worth, or your mad basketball skills on the pick-up court in your neighborhood park. However, if there are things you are experiencing that are bringing you joy and life and excitement, remember to share those things.

My 12 know all about my excitement for this book. I've shared about it not as a means of receiving affirmation, but as a way of expressing something that aligns with my passions, gifts and dreams. They hear about my gratitude for the teachers my kids have been fortunate to have, and they even hear about my latest house project that I'm working on, because these are things in which I find joy. Harmony and depth pour into our relationships when we're given opportunities to both weep and rejoice together.[32]

All this reality-sharing opens up space for others to do the same. Remember, we cannot be friends unless we know the ups and downs of each other's lives, the greatest struggles and deepest joys. These ABCs help us get to those deeper realities.

A couple of tips for sharing our realities:

Keep It Agenda-Free

This is about presence, not progress. We let God's Spirit do the progress part, and we rely on His Spirit to help us be present. His Spirit prompts us when to speak and when to stay quiet. We are not responsible to fix our 12. We are responsible to love them like Jesus loved His 12. We are not trying to manipulate behaviors that we want to see; rather, we are doing our best to guide others toward an obedience that they are sensing from God. The goal of loving our 12 is not only to teach them about Jesus' commands, it's to help them be obedient to the rule of Jesus in every area of their lives. When we see something that is out of alignment, we can speak up by sharing our reality, and give input, guidance and advice when others invite us to.

Be a Storyteller

Find ways to reflect and remember the many stories about how God is at work in your life. Scott and I have both found that journaling is helpful for retrieving stories we have reflected on. We have also experienced an uncanny number of times when something upon which we have recently reflected is given an opportunity to be told. I've often had conversations that begin with, "Today when I was reflecting..." or "Yesterday when I was journaling..." Finding a way to reflect and record your reality will go a long way in being able to readily access it for storytelling.

Storytelling is an art. You don't have to be the best at it, but you will get better the more you practice. Practice telling your reality. Soon you will start to learn the power of timing, when to speak up and when to shut up. You will learn to know when you've talked too long or when you've said too little. You will learn what details are needed and when you have overshared. This is taking steps with the Spirit, a partnership that requires some praying and discerning along the way. The next chapter will get into this even more.

Give Yourself Grace

No one's eternity or maturity is solely dependent on you. God is partnering with you, not giving you proprietary ownership of other people's destinies. Thank You, Jesus! Along the way, you will have moments where, at the end of the day, you will realize you've missed an opportunity to share your reality in a way that could have helped someone. You will also have times where you'll have a little bit of an authenticity-hangover, including the feeling that you've shared way too much. This is part of what it means to have faith, to trust that God will use those words to cultivate good in your life, others' lives and your shared lives together in community. Sometimes the gift of your story will not be well received. Some people might respond in ways that are hurtful and even mean. Please hear this: your stories have value not in being received, but in being lived. God's work in your life need only be validated by Him. If along the way you are blindsided by someone's ill response, know that God works for the good of those who love Him. You never know how or when your story might resonate or illuminate. Don't give up on your stories—practice again and again. Listen to the Spirit, trust in His work and practice.

Questions for Reflection and Discussion

1. How have you shared your reality with others?
2. Who has shared their reality with you? How did you receive it?
3. Which of the ABC's will be easiest for you to share? Which one is the hardest?

8

Spirit Fueled

"Awake my soul, awake my soul,
awake my soul. For you were
made to meet your maker."

– *Mumford & Sons,*
"Awake My Soul"

CHAPTER 8

INSUFFICIENTLY CHARGED

In 2012 my wife and I joined our close friends AJ and Rachel on a family trip to Texas. Some family friends of theirs had a hobby ranch they were eager to share with others, so we were invited to join the fun. We had only one child at the time, our 18-month-old son. We had lots of fun chasing chickens, petting goats and feeding horses. It was a needed break from the heavy and busy ministry life I had been accustomed to as a student pastor. One night we were out on the back patio watching the sun set and enjoying the drop in temperature as the scorching heat dissipated beyond the horizon. As we talked, our hosts asked poignant and personal questions that were getting to the root of what was becoming overwhelmingly tiring in our lives. I was, and for some time had been, teetering on the edge of a complete depletion of energy. It was AJ who made a comment that I'll never forget. As I shared about my "always on" mindset, he said, "Jake, you know what the problem is? It's not that you are busy. It's that as soon as God puts a drop in your bucket, you give it away." That statement is a long stretch from the kingdom ideal of how I believed I could be living my life. Loving others from the overflow of God's abundance was what I thought I was doing, but those closest to me knew it wasn't the case. Abundance was my theological stance, but depletion was my everyday reality. Since that day, I learned, sometimes the hard way, that living out of my own efforts will always leave me drained. I have been seeking to discover and align myself with the Spirit of God in such a way as to pour into others out of the overflow of God pouring into me.

Abundance is what Jesus promises we have through Him—life to the fullest. But a full life is not something we can achieve; it can't be earned. It is something given only through the Spirit of God through Jesus. It's also the only thing that will give us what we need to love our 12 like Jesus loved His 12. Without the abundant overflow of the Spirit in our lives, we simply will not make it with our 12. We will bail out or burn out.

Bailing and Burning Out

Bailing out and burning out are the end results of drifting in one of two directions. Bailing is the direction of relational withdrawal. It can take on many forms, from not returning phone calls, to making excuses or not showing up to social invitations. It's not just physical withdrawal, though. It can be withholding our reality. It can be putting up our guard just a little bit at a time until we find that some of our 12 don't actually know who we are. Withdrawing from socializing, serving or sharing are sure signs that we are drifting towards bailing on our 12. And it's also a sign that we are not seeking the abundant filling of Jesus' Spirit.

When living more out of depletion, rather than on dependency, I caught myself bailing on people who I honestly just didn't have the energy for. Fear that they would drain me of what little life I was surviving on would cause me to impose boundaries. Boundaries are important, but they can also become a self-justified tool for those of us who are living more out of self-reliance than on Spirit-reliance. In these instances, I didn't seek to hear from God about my response or His solutions; I just didn't have any margin in my life for another problem. So I crafted an over-spiritualized, boundary-laden excuse as to why I couldn't be involved.

Sometimes, we need to have healthy boundaries with our schedules and energies. As Christ-followers, those boundaries are not determined solely by our capacities. Loving our 12 comes from capacities that are received and revived through the Spirit of Jesus. None of us has the intention of bailing on our 12, but that is one of the directions we will head if we are driven by self-reliance. The other direction we will drift when driven by self-reliance is burnout.

Burnout is the default direction of our western culture. We are a diverse mix of self-reliant, self-determined, driven-toward-achievement cultures. We want to join the people of Babel, building our towers to reach the pinnacle of progress.[33] Burnout can be a bit of a buzzword while being, at the same time, taboo. It is worn as a badge of honor and shame. Those who have burned out and recovered will put it on their resume if it gets them that next promotion or job. Others who have experienced it and were never the same will tearfully, albeit sometimes reluctantly, speak of how they just couldn't cut it, maybe still can't. I'm convinced that burnout is an impending tidal wave gaining tremendous mass and velocity that will engulf emerging generations. Needless to say, followers of Christ are not immune to it.

I wasn't. Even after the warning more than ten years ago from AJ, I still drifted toward burnout. I still drift. Burnout is all but inevitable when we find ourselves depleted of our relational, mental or physical energy and at the same time find ourselves in situations where our core ideals are frustrated, recognition is withheld, or our calling is overshadowed by menial tasks. Immersion in the hustle, "fake-it-till-you-make-it" culture of America, alongside a sense of wanting to listen to Jesus and love others well, can easily put a follower of Jesus on a trajectory towards burnout unless it is fueled by Him. The end result of burnout is no better than bailing out: both leave us with little to offer our 12.

A Disciplined Life

When the disciples began to feel the pressures of growing a diverse movement, they sensed the need to bring others alongside them to help. One of the criteria they determined essential was being filled with the Spirit.[34] They were looking for partners in the mission that were Spirit-filled. The term *Spirit-filled* can can carry many connotations for different religious backgrounds. For the sake of our argument, we are saying *Spirit-filled* means that we depend solely on the Spirit to be equipped and empowered to do the work of Jesus in our world. We are using the phrase *Spirit-fueled* to attempt to capture the idea of both Spirit-filled and Spirit-activated. The Spirit is both the filler and the fuel for joining Jesus in His mission. Being in proximity to alignment with God's Spirit, however, is countercultural. To be in proximity to and in alignment with the person of the Spirit takes work, effort and discipline.

Having spiritual practices or disciplines does not mean we beckon God's Spirit like some genie that grants us wishes. There is always a risk that our relationship with God effectively turns into a series of transactions if we see our actions as "spiritual credits" we receive for going to church, reading our Bible, tithing and praying.

Socializing and serving are a greenhouse and sharing your reality is a fertilizer. Think of Spirit-fueling as pruning. It is the work of cutting out the things that prevent the fruit God promises from blooming in our lives.

This summer was my second year planting a garden. Last year, the tomatoes took over. This year it was the beans. The beans destroyed everything. Stalks wrapped themselves around everything they could find. The lettuce was all but choked out. The green peppers, dead. The beans spread and even overtook the lilies that weren't even in the garden.You would think the beans would be thriving, but they produced only one bean—and were killing everything else. They needed to be pruned long before they monopolized the entire garden. They needed to be shaped and encouraged to grow in a way that would allow both the beans and other plants the energy and room to bear fruit.

We like to measure growth, any growth. And we often mistake leaves for fruit. Leaves are not fruit.[35] This is a hard lesson for us. If something grows big or quickly, we celebrate it as successful. One of those heads of lettuce, before the beans got to it, grew three feet tall. It produced more lettuce than I could eat in a week if I ate it at every meal. But guess what? I wouldn't eat it. It was bitter. Fruit is as much about quality as it is quantity. Even if those beans had produced hundreds of pods, if they were bitter, sour or spoiled, the quantity wouldn't make a difference.

Our lives require the discipline of being shaped and pruned by God's Spirit so that we can have the abundance He promises. His abundance is as much about quality as quantity. It is good for me and others, and it's enough for me and others. If it's only good for only me, that's not the abundant life. If it's good enough for only me, that's not the abundant life. If it's good for others, and nothing is left for me, that's not abundance either—not God's abundance anyway.

Just a quick note that one of my greatest strengths is adaptability. Sometimes this comes off as flying by the seat of my pants, or in other words, being undisciplined. Discipline is not in my DNA. "Farm boy" Scott, on the other hand, has an internal alarm of 5:30 a.m., no matter the time zone. That doesn't mean that the disciplines we are about to explore have come easier for Scott than for me. In fact, I find it quite easy to engage in some, while others take a lot more work for me than for Scott.

Scott talks about these spiritual practices as prepping for spiritual heart surgery. It's getting into a position where God can do work on our souls. It's work that mends wounds, removes shrapnel, and reestablishes lifeblood. When you hear "spiritual disciplines," don't think about uncompromising routines. If that's what works for you, then go with it. If you are more like me, it might mean taking the practices and adapting them to times, places and experiences that fit your personality and passions. Make no mistake, however—they will require sacrifice, intentionality and change.

To kick us off, we'll start with one of Scott's biggest influences when it comes to spiritual disciplines: Richard Foster wrote what is now a classic book on spiritual disciplines. Here is Scott's summary of his book, *Celebration of Discipline*:

> *God has ordained 12 spiritual disciplines. These disciplines are the partnership between human effort and the indwelling Spirit to open our hearts for transformational change. The disciplines themselves do not produce change; they simply position us in a place where change can occur in the supernatural power of the Holy Spirit. Only the inner Spirit liberates us from the stifling service to our flesh. No amount of willpower or self-determination can purify our own heart.*

The 12 disciplines fall into three categories with four practices in each.

INWARD: Meditation, Prayer, Fasting and Study

OUTWARD: Simplicity, Solitude/Silence, Submission and Service

CORPORATE: Confession, Worship, Guidance and Celebration

Each of these disciplines has power and merit and is worth a more in-depth exploration. If you're comfortable and understand each of them, we would suggest choosing one from each category that stretches your dependence on God a little more. If this is new to you, it might be worth learning a little more about each discipline, perhaps even reading through Foster's book. You might also have noticed how some of these disciplines have influenced the practices we have set forth in this book. But we think one discipline is worth discussing more at length. The greatest potential to redirect us against the rush and rush, hyper-hustle culture is the practice of silence and solitude.

An Ever-Present Danger

A few summers ago our family went on a little jet ski ride on one of those three-person Sea-Doo watercrafts. We creatively maneuvered our family of five onto the floating death trap. I say floating death trap because that is what my three children thought it was. It took all that we had to convince them to just go in slow figure-eights around the shallows of the bay. We left the safety of the beach as I puttered along at a few miles per hour. Slowly, I made my way into deeper waters, careful not to let the waves of our own wake cause too much of a scare. After a few minutes, we were all having fun, laughing as we crashed over waves. Of course, being the great dad I am, I had been slowly increasing the acceleration and making more thrilling turns. I couldn't tell you exactly when things went wrong, or how. I do know that one of the waves was a lot bigger than I had anticipated, and we were going a little faster into the turn on the previous passes. I found myself clinging tightly to the handles as my two boys and wife grasped my life vest with all their might—and weight. I could feel us all leaning toward the dark water, and I knew that unless I did something, we would soon all go overboard. The problem was that the handle I clung to so tightly just happened to be the throttle. The more their weight pulled me backward, the harder I pulled on that throttle. As the jet ski accelerated and my children screamed, I had only one option. I let go. (I also pulled my daughter, who was sitting in front of me, off the Sea-Doo.) I wasn't sure what was going to happen, but the last thing I wanted was a heavy watercraft landing on her. In the end, everyone was fine. Perhaps the kids were not 100 percent aware that the engine stopped and that all would be okay. We may have had to deal with some screaming and tears and declarations that they would never, ever ride a Sea-Doo again.

This is my life a lot of the time. Maybe yours, too. We have our hands on the throttle, and we are doing our best just to hang on and not dump everything and everyone into the dark unknown of the tumultuous surroundings we are trying to navigate.

Just me?

Life is moving so fast, is so loud and so chaotic, that little margin remains for anything slow, quiet and simple. We hang on for dear life, and as we do, we seem to also be laying on the throttle. If you remember, the Jesus-strategy is slow, simple, small and sustainable. To work against the current of our world that sets us so easily adrift, we would encourage this two-pronged practice as the most pressing for our time.

C. S. Lewis says it well in *Mere Christianity*:

> "It comes the very moment you wake up each morning. All your wishes and hopes for the day rush at you like wild animals. And the first job each morning consists simply in shoving them all back; in listening to that other voice, taking that other point of view, letting that other larger, stronger, quieter life come flowing in. And so on, all day. Standing back from all your natural fussings and frettings; coming in out of the wind."

Silence and Solitude

Silence and solitude is about reserving time and space to push back the wild animals. It might be every morning before your feet hit the floor. It might be hitting your knees as soon as your feet hit the floor, or during the 20-minute commute to work. It could be your walk or run, or the time you sip your coffee in the morning. It doesn't have to be morning, although mornings seem to work for a great number of people. Silence and solitude is about pushing out the noise and distraction that surround us and so easily entangles us to seek uninterrupted stillness instead—stillness of our bodies, our heavy minds and even heavier hearts.

Jesus often went to secluded places and spent time hearing from God.[36] This is how He was filled and fueled for the work ahead of Him. Even before starting His public ministry, Jesus spent 40 days in seclusion and solitude. Those days in the desert solidified His identity and empowered His ministry. We see in the narratives of His life that Jesus was constantly pressed by people to teach and heal. He spent most of everyday, all day, with His closest followers. He had little down time and even less alone time. Spiritual refueling through silence and solitude was crucial for Jesus.

In one of those seasons where I seemed to be running on all cylinders, and yet was not redlining my life, I developed a practice of "holy napping." I'm not sure that is what it is called, and it may sound sacrilegious or lazy to some, but for me it was an essential part of filling and fueling through the Spirit. Without a nap on my most energy-consuming days I would end up exhausted, sometimes with migraines that would immobilze me the next day. So on the busiest days, the most demanding of days, I cut time out of my schedule, a day packed from 8 a.m. until after 10 p.m., to slow down, actually stop, and be still. I would lie on a couch and take deep breaths and then surrender all my cares and anxiety to Jesus. I would ask Him to take the racing thoughts about a message I was working on, or a meeting that didn't go well, or even a meeting I was afraid would not go well, and I would say, "It's Yours." Then I would sit in silence, listening to my own breath or the sounds of the wind outside. Sometimes I would fall asleep. If I did, it was usually for less than fifteen minutes. In that time, I would often be stirred with vivid images and ideas, alongside an enthusiastic rush of fresh air that would cause me to feel more refreshed than even a full night's sleep. In those times I might have a new perspective about a conversation, an idea I had never considered, or a conviction that was previously waning. Almost always I was reinvigorated for the work ahead of me. Those times of silence and solitude became a baseline for other times for me. Those days taught me how to do a similar practice when I started doing Scripture reading, meditation and journaling. Those "holy naps" were foundational for helping me understand how to to empty myself of my anxieties and agendas.

A few years after implementing this "holy napping," I heard the author Mike Breen talk about working from a place of rest versus resting from work. This is the natural God-graced rhythm that we find in the creation narrative. The first thing humanity experienced was a day of rest with the creator.[37] This is in stark contrast to the pattern of the world. The pattern of the world would have us conform to living for the weekend, the next day off, or the next vacation. Silence and solitude helped me develop a mindset of seeing rest as the first thing I do. It becomes a way to offer our bodies as living sacrifices to God, so that we might discover how He is at work and how He wills us to join Him.

A confession now: I don't do "holy naps" anymore. Now they are just normal naps. Some of that comes from a season of chronic sleep deprivation; perhaps they are still holy, but they are few and far between. On occasion, I do take prayer walks in a nature center or along a trail. If I find a secluded spot with a bench or a nice patch of grass, I'll lie down and do what I used to do, closing my eyes and seeking to get a sense of the Spirit of God at work. "Holy naps," prayer walks in nature preserves, and even "prayer sits" in my backyard have helped me learn to tell the difference between my own desires and desires that have the same shape as God's dreams. The practice of silence and solitude helps shape our desires and dreams, and the way we try to make them a reality, to be congruent with God's. I have also learned to be leery of big dreams, also known as "God-sized dreams," because they are often deterrents from a Jesus-model mission and strategy. When my dreams are about scale rather than congruence, they almost always move me from a posture of being a servant to one that requires the services of others around me. They almost always end up building my empire rather than God's kingdom.

When Scott talks about his time of spiritual refueling through silence and solitude, he speaks of it as a requirement. He said it's essential for survival. Without it, he just won't make it. He's right; we won't make it. Scott's rhythms are a little more predictable than my own. Where I might sprinkle in two or three times a week of extended silence and solitude, Scott doesn't go a day without it. He wakes up early, puts his headphones in (I know that doesn't sound like silence, but it quiets the voices and pushes back the distractions that echo in the chambers of his mind) and reads through Scripture. After a time of reflections and prayer, he writes out what he is feeling and what he is sensing God is trying to communicate. This thirty minutes to an hour each day is what keeps Scott going. It's what keeps him dependent on God and committed to his 12.

The key is not to do what Scott and I are doing—or what anyone else is doing for that matter—when it comes implementing spiritual practices. The key is that you do whatever is necessary to stay dependent on God's Spirit, doing everything necessary to maintain that connection and gain greater connection. That might be an everyday thing, an every-other-day thing, or even a once-a-week thing. Longer than once a week sounds unsustainable; a week is a long time to go without seeking the presence of someone you love and desire to be close to.

What will it take for you to be in the best position to sustain an abundant life that can overflow to your 12 (and others)?

What will keep your tank full?

The point is not to live a life that swings back and forth between empty and full, but rather a life that lives closer to spill-over than depletion. Know yourself well enough to recognize when you begin to move from Spirit-reliance to self-dependence. Jesus knew when His physical, mental and spiritual energies were being used; and He adjusted accordingly. Beyond what your week looks like, it may also be wise to consider doing extended times monthly, quarterly and yearly.

Another reason we are big on making silence and solitude a priority now is that it is an easy way to engage in other disciplines. Think about how these activities can link with silence and solitude:

- Inward disciplines of fasting, meditation, prayer, study
- Creative expression/celebration
- Connect to creation
- Writing confessions and encouragement
- Listen to teaching and preaching

Find the means and time to make silence and solitude a spiritual discipline. Doing so will fuel your spirit and your mission of loving your 12.

Results

When we prioritize our 12 and put into practice the activities suggested in this book, we will find ourselves compelled towards practices that help us become Spirit-fueled. Joining Jesus in His mission through His methods drives us to seek encounters with God. Perhaps one of the reasons a great many Christ-followers today struggle with doing what is commonly labeled as devotions or quiet time is because of a lack of engagement in the mission of Jesus. When we are primarily concerned with a personalized faith that is geared toward and caters to preferences, we feel far less compelled to pursue activities that require challenge, change and surrender. When faith by-products are spoon-fed to me, I have little incentive to feed myself. Being an everyday follower of Jesus (who has others to pour into) engages us with the mission in a whole new way and can be a powerful motivator for us to seek after God's Spirit.

If you sense a reluctancy within you to connect with Jesus in a way that activates His Spirit in your life, there is also a chance that the Jesus you have been worshiping and claiming allegiance to isn't the Jesus we meet in the Scriptures. The results of accepting or receiving a Jesus that meets our needs and doesn't expect participation beyond static rituals within yourself, does not elicit the kind of dependency we see Jesus model. A Jesus that makes us happy as long as we stay relatively well-behaved has little more to offer than what has already been given. This kind of Jesus does not need to be sought out until our equation of "good behavior = happiness and health" is no longer working. Even then, little more is needed than a quotable platitude that we give a whirl for a few months. If you're wondering if the Jesus you met is the Jesus who promises to be with you as you go and love others the way He loved His others, then ask Him now. Ask Him now to give what He promised: His very Spirit. It is His Spirit that was promised to comfort and to guide, to fill and to fuel you, to bring abundance of a fruitful, undiminishing, untainted life that overflows to others. Just ask—He freely gives.

Questions for Reflection and Discussion

1. How do you re-fuel with His Spirt?
2. How do you feel when you are not connected with God?
3. Who in your life stays "spirit-fueled"? What disciplines do they employ in their life to avoid "bailing and burning out"?

9

Send

"Jesus' friends are in no way remarkable for their talent or character. He who considers the apostles or disciples great from a human or religious point of view raises the suspicion that he is unacquainted with true greatness. Moreover, he is confusing standards, for the apostle and disciple have nothing to do with such greatness. Their uniqueness consists of their being sent, of their God-given role of pillars for the coming salvation."

—Romano Guardini, *The Lord*

*

CHAPTER 9

Think about how you feel when you receive marketing from one of your favorite stores or restaurants with a really good deal or coupon. One of those half-off kind of deals. Think about how excited you get, and how you start thinking about how to use it. Now think about how it feels when you notice that little symbol hanging inconspicuously behind the bold writing. The asterisk.

50% OFF*

And so you read the small print . . .

*Exclusions apply

It's typically an exclusion for the very things I most want to get. The brand of shoes I buy, the day of the week I would have gone, the entree I would have ordered. It's even worse if we go to use it, only to find out about the exclusions after the fact.

Some of us that have been told there's an asterisk after Jesus' words to His followers about joining Him in His mission.

We read and hear the famed "Great Commission" words of Jesus like this:

> Therefore (*you**) go and make disciples of all nations, baptizing them in the name of the Father and of the Son and of the Holy Spirit, and teaching them to obey everything I have commanded *you**. And surely I am with *you** always, to the very end of the age."

*You** equals followers of Jesus that are mature. *The ones who have their act together. *The ones who make no visible mistakes. *The ones who have no doubts. *The ones who have the greatest leadership potential. *Those who are good public speakers. *Those who are socially most likeable. *Those who know all the words to all the songs and hymns. *Those who have read the Bible cover to cover—twice. *Those who have at least 100 Bible verses memorized. *Those who have graduated from Jesus-school magna cum laude.

You get the idea.

The exclusions after the asterisks that have been inserted into Jesus' words could be endless. We have all sorts of ideas about what qualifies and disqualifies people for or from living this command.

Jesus' invitation to partner with Him, to have a co-mission with Him, does not include any exclusions. There are no exclusions for those who can hear and receive the message of new life in Christ and desire to learn how to live under His rule, and there are no exclusions for those of His followers being sent by Him.

The word *mission* comes from a word that means "to be sent" or "sent one." Sending isn't just something God does; it is a part of His very nature. Just as Jesus was sent by God into our existence...just as the Spirit was sent by the Son and the Father, Jesus' followers are now sent with His Spirit into the world.

We are sent.

And so are our 12.

There is no asterisk beside Jesus' words. There are no disqualifications. There are no exclusions to what has been coined "The Great Commission." To us, it's more like the "The Great Co-Mission." We have been entrusted and given authority to participate *with* Jesus in His mission.

So just to be clear:
There are NO EXCLUSIONS.

Not even the one you just said in your mind. Or the one you heard from someone else.

NO EXCLUSIONS. NO DISQUALIFIERS.

"What about....?"

Nope, not even that.

Just before Jesus gives His parting instructions, we see in the narrative a clue as to who gets to partner with Jesus. It's in the verses that get excluded from our quotes that key us into the non-exclusionary reality of Jesus' final command.

Here is the context:

> *Then the eleven disciples went to Galilee, to the mountain where Jesus had told them to go. When they saw him, they worshiped him; but some doubted. Then Jesus came to them and said, 'All authority in heaven and on earth has been given to me.'* (Matthew 28:16-18)

Jesus is handing the mission over to His 12. (Well, now 11, because Judas betrayed Him and then killed himself.) Jesus is essentially saying to the disciples, "It's your turn. It's your turn to join in." And in that group, some worshiped Him . . .

And . . .

Some . . .

Doubted.

Doubt did not disqualify the disciples from becoming disciple-makers. And doubt does not disqualify anyone in your 12. The first disciples didn't have it all figured out. Heck, they weren't even positive they fully believed what was happening, and yet that didn't stop Jesus from offering them a partnership with Him in the mission.

Our 12 are sent on a journey of selecting 12 of their own, socializing and serving, sharing their reality, and refueling their souls. Our 12 can join Jesus in the co-mission of loving others like He has loved. Our 12 are not disqualified. They are a great reminder that neither are you.

Your 12 are part of the co-mission, even if they are young. Even if they are immature. Even if they don't know the books of the Bible or even own a Bible. No label, identification or preference renders anyone as ineligible. No one is too new to faith, too biblically illiterate or too imperfect to keep from participating in the primary objective given to Jesus' followers. In fact, it is in participating that our 12 will likely grow the most. Participation in the cause breeds purpose, and purpose breeds passion. This passion will lead to a stronger desire to participate in what is typically seen as precursors to being sent. We don't withhold the opportunity to participate in the mission from those who haven't learned enough of the Bible yet, haven't attended programing and Sunday services enough, or haven't given a high enough percentage of their income to the organized church. Perhaps the reason we find so many followers of Jesus educated beyond their obedience[38] is that they have been wrongly disqualified from this most basic and foundational command.

One of the reasons Jesus was unflinching in His invitation, despite doubts, is that He wasn't going to leave them alone. The Great Commission is truly a co-mission with Him. It is not picking up where He left off, but joining Him where He invites us in. He promised His followers that He would be with them until this age, the one we are in right now, comes to an end. We see later that "with" isn't just an "alongside of" promise, but a "within" promise. The Spirit of Jesus is sent to indwell the very heart and soul of those who call Him Ruler and Rescuer. Jesus, with us through His Spirit, is what gives us the boldness, endurance, wisdom and patience to love our 12 like Jesus loved His.

When to Send

When our 12 begin to orient their lives toward learning to live under the rule and rescue of Jesus, they are qualified to be sent. We cannot wait for them to get their spiritual act together and live up to our standard of maturity. This mindset has led to our current situation. Rather than take Jesus up on the challenge to go be disciple-making disciples, many opt for more consumption of religious goods. This has left the vast majority of followers ill-equipped for a Jesus-modeled form of discipleship. When confronted with His challenge, they feel that more training, learning or time is needed. We have been left with a wholly unfit group of disciples who have failed to participate. Few followers of Jesus even seem to have knowledge of this invitation of Jesus to join Him in mission.

Maturity isn't the qualifier for participation. Participation is what helps us become mature. **When our 12 begin to love their 12 like Jesus loved His 12, they will grow.** Following Jesus will take on a new meaning when our 12 have been unleashed to find their own 12. When our 12 begin to show spiritual receptivity to Jesus not just as a good teacher or good person, but as ruler and rescuer of their lives, they adopt the same character of sentness we have received from Jesus.

The Deep End of the Pool

When I was younger, I was fascinated with the deep end of the pool. All I wanted to do was get permission to swim in the deep end, to be able to go off the diving board and water slides, and to dive down to pick up quarters and dimes thrown by my brother. I remember that at camps and water parks, you needed to pass the test to go in the deep end. A lifeguard would watch as you swam unassisted from one side of the pool to the other, treaded water for 30 seconds, or whatever the test was. After the test, you received a wristband clearing you for admittance. If you did not pass, you were confined to the shallow end with the splashing toddlers wearing floaties around their arms.

For most of my Christ-following journey, I was under the impression that disciple-making was like the deep end of the pool, where you had to pass a certain test to be able to participate. You had to prove yourself. The test seemed to always be different depending who I was with, but I've come to realize that the deep end isn't where the disciple-making happens. Discipleship and disciple-making are about the whole pool. Jesus doesn't say, "All authority has been given to me...Pop quiz time! Let's see how well you can do!" He says, "Jump in."

Wait, you might say. The disciples spent three years with Jesus—three years of close, intimate learning and living with Jesus.

But that's not what qualified them. That's what made them friends.

Followers of Jesus, including the 12, were participating in the mission long before they had any qualifications, and in a much shorter time than three years. It is recorded in the narrative about Jesus written by Luke. The disciples were sent out by Jesus to the towns to perform miracles and proclaim the Kingdom of God. It seems Jesus had His followers doing cannonballs before He taught them to swim.

Questions for Reflection and Discussion

1. How do you feel unqualified to start your journey to 12?
2. Are there other barriers to your journey to 12?

10

Imagine

"Because when you are
imagining, you might as well
imagine something worthwhile."

– Lucy Maud Montgomery,
Anne of Green Gables

IMAGINE

Imagine if every follower of Jesus, just in the U.S., devoted themselves to invest in Just 12. The numbers would be staggering, the effects even more so.

The U.S. currently has almost 330 million people. Professing followers of Jesus make up about 65% of those people. Potentially every person in the U.S. could be in someone's 12. The spiritual landscape of the U.S. would change tomorrow if even half the professing followers of Jesus found Just 12.

Theories rarely work out on paper, and investing in 12 isn't going to happen for everyone. Some of us might have four or five people in our journey towards 12. And, in all likelihood, some people might be in more than one person's 12. Remember, Just 12 is about striving to love well, not fill a quota. This isn't some Jesus pyramid scheme we are advocating. We do want to see our country and world changed, but Just 12 isn't about conquering the world. It's about 12—my 12 and your 12. Just 12 is about changing *your* world before it's about changing *the* world.

If every follower of Jesus is committed to this Jesus-modeled strategy, the world would quickly see Christians increasing engagement in their faith. More people would be striving to love like Jesus. More people would experience being loved by Jesus.

Think about what this model does for families.

Husbands will be investing in their wives, and wives in their husbands ...not just to survive the challenges of marriage, but to build each other up to reflect the image of Jesus. Fathers and mothers will be the primary influence in their children's spirituality and help form them into followers of Jesus. The direction of a family will be about more than whether a father goes to church or not. No longer will the spiritual influence of parents be about choosing the right church based on cultural preferences of worship or preaching. It will be about the trajectory of the whole family toward becoming and making transforming learners under the rule of Jesus.

Think about what this does for friendship and "accountability."

Imagine a world where every follower is prioritizing two or three friendships with fellow "iron sharpening" followers. The not-so-easily-broken strand of three cords spoken about in the Hebrew Scriptures[39] is not an aspirational goal, but an intentional investment in the strategy of Just 12. It is no longer necessary to add an accountability small group to an already busy schedule when authenticity is being shared in the relational model of Jesus.

Think of the disadvantaged and disenfranchised.

When everyone has Just 12, and there is room in the 12 for the least and the lost and the lonely, then the least, lost and lonely become outdated labels. The plagues of anxiety, depression and loneliness will receive an inoculation that gives a chance for hope to take hold. The viruses of injustice, prejudice and racism will get a dose of disinfectant that diminishes the dividing lines that have prevailed for far too long. The sicknesses of partisanship, polarization and preferential treatment will be faced with a regimen of listening, understanding and connection. The diseases of judgment, self-righteousness and self-justification will be cleansed with the same self-sacrificial love of Jesus.

Let's say it again. If each of us commits to Just 12, our collective effort will be a major factor in combating the biggest social crises our nation currently faces, or will face.

What other strategy can change whole nations? What other strategy can change the world? What other strategy can make a noticeable impact on your local community? We've yet to see another strategy have the power and longevity like this strategy of Jesus. Granted, Jesus' strategy does come with a heck of a lot of good news. Still, the simple, slow, small, sustainable, Jesus-modeled strategy can change the world because it has and is. It's not a strategy that has at times made a difference in the world; it's a strategy that continues to make the world a different place.

What other strategy offers an alternative to the church in the U.S. that's making decisions based on financial pressures and bureaucratic business practices?

What other strategy moves followers of Jesus toward living out the command of loving our enemies so intentionally and tangibly?

What other strategy has such great potential for every suffering person to have someone to go to in their deepest time of need? What other strategy cultivates so many conversations across race, politics, sexuality, gender, class and generations?

Imagine that the non-religious, those turned away and turned off from Christianity, aren't being berated with arguments, or pestered into church buildings, but are instead being included in the lives of people who love Jesus. Imagine that they are loved and shown love that is detached from any institutional mandate or organizational agenda.

Are you having a hard time imagining? Why is that?

Some of us struggle to have an imagination for this because we have something to lose in our current models and strategies. It's possible that some of us are afraid to lose influence or power or, in some cases, money. Lack of imagination can usually be tied to idolatry and loyalties to the status quo. Our commitment to the conventional prevents us from seeing other possibilities. Our current structures and strategies blind us from alternatives that require not-so-small shifts in thinking and acting. When we have much to lose, we have little to imagine.

A Jesus-modeled strategy is the only sustainable strategy. These strategies have proven through generations and across cultures to be the only strategies that deliver on the mandate that everyday followers of Jesus engage in the mission and message of Jesus in everyday ways.

The current strategies being employed by the majority of churches in the U.S., and many other parts of the world that are following suit, don't have the mobility or the ability to engage the masses. They don't have the low cost (no cost) and low bureaucracy that a Just 12 strategy has.

When we re-engage this strategy of Jesus, to focus on Just 12, we can participate in the movement of Jesus that is not manufactured. Politics, policies, programs, productions, power plays or payrolls cannot do what practicing the strategy of Jesus can do. It's time we stop throwing so much time, energy, effort and resources toward what is yielding such little results for the Kingdom. The problem is not a lack of effort to change the spiritual landscape in the U.S. The problem is a lack of strategy. It's time for a shift.

Questions for Reflection and Discussion

1. What would happen in the U.S. if every person would be in someone's 12?
2. How would you change if you prioritized 12 others?

11

Shift

"Some people don't like change,
but you need to embrace change
if the alternative is disaster."

–*ELON MUSK*

CHAPTER 11

WHERE DO WE GO FROM HERE?

We set out to write this book out of a desire for everyone who follows after Jesus to sense a spark to re-engage with Him. But not as a good person doing good-person things. We desire that everyday followers of Jesus would start to live the strategy that Jesus demonstrated and commanded. For many of us, this is a huge shift in thinking, and that shift will not come for most of us without a shift in action. In other words, the best way to make the shift isn't more study, more academic research or more participation in organizational programs. The best way to make the shift is to make the shift. It's to start loving up to 12 people that God has put in your life. The shift means you start making some selections, you continue to socialize and serve, you take steps of vulnerability and authenticity, and you share your reality. The shift means refueling your soul for mission, not just self-care and development. The shift means sending those who you are pouring into to pour into others. Just like Jesus did.

The Just 12 shift does not require permission or special training. Letting your pastor in on what you are up to might not be a bad idea; they will likely be encouraged and energized by your intentionality. But you don't need to go through any leadership board to start doing this. The permission has already been given by Jesus. As uncomfortable as it may seem, this shift comes with on-site, in-time training. It's training that comes when you need it—in the Spirit's timing. It's training that will send you into solitude and silence and cause you to desperately seek the Scriptures. When you start your Just 12 journey, you will find yourself seeking answers to questions you didn't even know you had. The journey will lead you to deeper times of worship and more reflective times of Scripture meditation. It will also lead you to lean heavily on the two or three iron-sharpening friends in your 12. Do you see how this simple strategy aligns with God's Spirit to form, reform and transform our character and identity? As we pursue our 12 as Jesus did, we will gain a passion for the things of Jesus and His Kingdom. The guilt/shame-ridden cycle of religion will be replaced with a compulsion to participate with God. No longer will we need to be enticed, inspired or, worse yet, coerced to participate in spiritual practices. Obligation and ritual will be replaced with yearning and anticipation.

Never Shift Alone

This journey has been one that Scott and I have shared and continue to share. Although the speed of change and the intersections of enlightenment have been different, we nonetheless have sojourned toward this new (old) way of making disciple-makers. We would encourage that you have others on your journey as well. Not just those who may be in your 12, but two or three others who are asking similar questions and seeking similar answers.

Many of you reading this book will have a connection to a local church, but many of you will not. For those of you who have, for whatever reason, found yourself on the outside of an organized church, you do need community. If a group of people rallying around this strategy can become your community, we want to help foster that. Find Just12 on social media, and start commenting and sharing your experience. Your questions, challenges and successes will add more than just content to the conversation—it will bring camaraderie to the cause. We hope everyone engages this way, but especially those who long for a spiritual community and have been unable to find it.

Anyone can reach out to us using the information below. If you find yourself struggling with a topic, feeling defeated, or you want to share an encouraging or profound experience relating to your 12, please let us know. We both have families and commitments, but we will do our best to respond. We would love to help everyone get started on this journey and answer questions/concerns/struggles you are feeling. We have had many of them ourselves. You're not alone.

Scott: just12.scottk@gmail.com

Jake: just12.jake@gmail.com

Those Who Have Gone Ahead

Not long ago Scott planned and started hosting Just 12 retreats. Scott has shifted the vision of his church to equipping and encouraging 300 disciple-makers by 2030. The church is shifting away from growing a gathering or having a certain amount of givers or leaders. Remember the strategy is slow, small, simple and sustainable. Scott plans to measure his success by how many people go through the Just 12 retreats that he (and others) will lead two to three times a year. A few people from those retreats shared a little about their journey.

"I was feeling pretty down for being on this journey and not even being able to identify a few people to begin my 12 journey with. One day I prayed for God to reveal to me who he wants in my twelve. The next week, I was scrambling to find some product for my store and, out of desperation, I called my old store. They had it—but it was much farther away than the other closest 30 or so stores. After a very long and stressful day, I got in my car and drove to my old store. Once I got there, I saw Ryan sitting in the lobby eating some tacos he bought for the team. It was around 10 p.m., closing time, and Ryan was the opening shift (4:30 a.m.-1 p.m.), so I thought it was weird he was still there. Of course, not to God's surprise, I was able to sit down and share some extra tacos and guac with Ryan. After catching up on each other's lives, it was clear that God was prompting me to have Ryan in my 12. The mere fact that he brought tacos and came to visit my old store for the first time in three months on the same day and the same time as me being there seemed like more than a coincidence. It's not always a tangible voice or a "holy" feeling that you get from God, but it's the subtle things…"

–Sean, Coffeeshop Store Manager

"My 12 consists of my family and friends and those that need to have hope and know God's love. I'm purposefully making a conscious effort to be a presence in their lives. It has been as simple as a text, phone call, note or meeting for coffee."

–Sarajo, Accountant

What we have noticed from those who have started this journey is the discovery for many that the mission of Jesus is more accessible than what they were accustomed to believe. What has happened for several others is that Just 12 has given permission to "count" what they were already doing. Engagement of faith is moving outside of the building and away from attendance. It's moving toward everyday followers participating in everyday ways of loving like Jesus.

Groups

Some of you are already part of organized groups where reading and discussing Just 12 would be a simple way to gain some traction and movement. You will notice that each chapter has a set of questions for discussion. They are a launching point that we hope gets to some of the questions and struggles we were having that led us to this book. Your group could take it a step further and commit to not only reading and studying the book, but each finding your Just 12 together. Think for a moment about what your group would be like if you had already made this shift. What would discussions and gatherings be like? What topics would need to be brought up and learned? Just 12 could be a powerful catalyst for a group to move the dial on engaging with Jesus in the comission into which He has invited us.

Church and Ministry Leaders

Many pastors that have been part of this conversation have been interested in making a shift, while at the same time hesitant because of the implications of systemic change it could bring. The first step is the same for all of us: start with a few people in your 12.

Some additional experiences will help make a shift if you are a church or ministry leader.

- Begin or join a cohort
- Challenge your staff or coworkers to start Just 12
- Lead a Just 12 retreat
- Join a group of pastors for a retreat in Colorado

Several pastors have begun organizing or hosting regional pastors' cohorts. Just 12 can be a catalyst for other topics for discussion and support. Cohorts exploring the broader issues surrounding the decline of Christianity in America, the state of the global church, or redefining success will serve to strengthen the framework needed for churches to make the shift to Just 12.

Leaders can also challenge staff to a Just 12 vision in preparing for an organizational shift. If there is any validity in this strategy, it will rattle some of the institutionalized foundations to which we have become accustomed. As mentioned above, Scott has already been making this shift at his church. Both of us would be glad to coach others who are ready—or walk alongside you as you get ready. If you would like to start leading your own Just 12 retreat, retreat guides are available. They can be used as-is or customized to your style and needs.

In this process, we have also discovered a huge need for safe places for leaders to rest and reset. For those of you who need such a place, we invite you to join us for a leader retreat in the hills of Colorado. A generous couple has built a ranch where groups of us can gather to learn from each other, and perhaps unlearn together. Ten percent of the proceeds of this book will go to fund travel scholarships for these retreats. (All other proceeds will fund training and coaching for churches and groups toward a Just 12 strategy). For more details on our next retreat, reach out to Scott or Jake using the contact info listed earlier. If you have read this far, the reality is that we would just love to say thank you and hear your feedback.

Questions for Reflection and Discussion

1. What's a tangible next step for you?
2. Who could you receive encouragement from to take this next step with?

12

Your 12

CHAPTER 12

YOUR 12

When we set out to write this book, we had no intention of having 12 chapters. We have added and taken away chapters. As we were brainstorming the last chapters of the book, it was Scott's daughter who said, "Oh, you are going to have 12 chapters...Just 12 chapters?" Although it seems like cheating that this chapter is basically a blank page, we think it makes a whole lot of sense that we would end this way. After all, in the parting words of Jesus, which are the premise of this whole book, He essentially leaves it up to His followers to keep the movement moving. And so we leave with that same attitude.

All authority in heaven and earth has been given to Jesus Christ, the risen ruler and rescuer of the world. As He said to His first followers, He says to us and to you:

It's your turn.

1. _____

2. _____

3. _____

4. _____

5. _____

6. _____

7. _____

8. _____

9. _____

10. _____

11. _____

12. _____

End Notes

[1] Matthew 16:19 I will give you the keys of the kingdom of heaven; whatever you bind on earth will be bound in heaven, and whatever you loose on earth will be loosed in heaven.

[2] Alan Hirsh and Dave Fegusen wrote the book "On the Verge," and we were immersed in the content. Hirsch was also an adjunct faculty where Jake did his graduate work. An associate of Hirsh through Forge Network, Kim Hammond, joined us on staff and had a tremendous impact on our thinking and practices. Mike Frost was featured at several events, and his BELLS practices helped birth the missional practices employed at our church.

[3] This alludes to what happened when the message about Jesus was first shared publicly. Acts 2:41 "Those who accepted his message were baptized, and about three thousand were added to their number that day."

[4] Barnes, Rebecca, and Lindy Lowry. "7 Startling Facts: An Up Close Look at Church Attendance in America." ChurchLeaders. Outreach Magazine, April 10, 2018. https://churchleaders.com/pastors/pastor-articles/139575-7-startling-facts-an-up-close-look-at-church-attendance-in-america.html.

[5] "Five Trends Defining Americans' Relationship to Churches." Barna.com. Barna Group, February 19, 2020. https://www.barna.com/research/current-perceptions/.

[6] "2018 Online Giving Statistics, Trends & Data: The Ultimate List of Giving Stats." Nonprofits Source, December 2018. https://nonprofitssource.com/online-giving-statistics/.

[7] "In U.S., Decline of Christianity Continues at Rapid Pace." Pew Research Center's Religion & Public Life Project, October 17, 2019. https://www.pewforum.org/2019/10/17/in-u-s-decline-of-christianity-continues-at-rapid-pace/.

[8] "Church Dropouts Have Risen to 64%-But What About Those Who Stay?" Barna.com. Barna Group, September 2019. https://www.barna.com/research/resilient-disciples/.

[9] Publication. American Worldview Inventory 2020 – At a Glance. Glendale, AZ: Arizona Christian University, 2020.

[10] Carter, Joe. "The U.S. Sends—and Receives—More Christian Missionaries Than Any Other Country." The Gospel Coalition, February 20, 2012. https://www.thegospelcoalition.org/article/the-u-s-sends-and-receives-more-christian-missionaries-than-any-other-count/.

[11] Henderson, Jim, and Matt Casper. Essay. In Jim and Casper Go to Church: Frank Conversation about Faith, Churches, and Well-Meaning Christians, 147–48. Carol Stream, Ill: BarnaBooks, 2007.

[12] John 13:34 A new command I give you: Love one another. As I have loved you, so you must love one another.

[13] John 20:21 Again Jesus said, "Peace be with you! As the Father has sent me, I am sending you.

[14] Matthew 28:19 Therefore go and make disciples of all nations, baptizing

them in the name of the Father and of the Son and of the Holy Spirit

[15] Philippians 2:3-4 Do nothing out of selfish ambition or vain conceit. Rather, in humility value others above yourselves, not looking to your own interests but each of you to the interests of the others.

[16] John 15:15 I no longer call you servants, because a servant does not know his master's business. Instead, I have called you friends, for everything that I learned from my Father I have made known to you.

[17] Ecclesiastes 4:12 Though one may be overpowered, two can defend themselves. A cord of three strands is not quickly broken.

[18] John 15:15 I no longer call you servants, because a servant does not know his master's business. Instead, I have called you friends, for everything that I learned from my Father I have made known to you.

[19] Referring to the transfiguration found in Matthew 17:1–8, Mark 9:2–8, Luke 9:28–36

[20] Grigg, Ty. "How I Learned to Stop Worrying About the Billy Graham Rule and Love Like Jesus." Missio Alliance, August 11, 2020. https://www.missioalliance.org/how-i-learned-to-stop-worrying-about-the-billy-graham-rule-and-love-like-jesus/.

[21] Don't stop meeting together with other believers, which some people have gotten into the habit of doing. Instead, encourage each other, especially as you see the day drawing near. Hebrews 10:25

[22] Greater love has no one than this: to lay down one's life for one's friends. John 15:13

[23] Everly, George S. "How to Pull Away from Toxic People, and Who to Replace Them With." Psychology Today. Sussex Publishers, November 24, 2019. https://www.psychologytoday.com/us/blog/when-disaster-strikes-inside-disaster-psychology/201911/how-pull-away-toxic-people-and-who.

[24] Acts 9:3-4 And as he journeyed, he came near Damascus: and suddenly there shone round about him a light from heaven: And he fell to the earth, and heard a voice saying unto him, Saul, Saul, why persecutest thou me?

[25] Philipians 2:12-13 Therefore, my dear friends, as you have always obeyed—not only in my presence, but now much more in my absence—continue to work out your salvation with fear and trembling, for it is God who works in you to will and to act in order to fulfill his good purpose.

[26] 1 Thessalonians 5:19-22 Do not quench the Spirit. Do not treat prophecies with contempt but test them all; hold on to what is good, reject every kind of evil.

[27] 1 Timothy 4:16 Watch your life and doctrine closely. Persevere in them, because if you do, you will save both yourself and your hearers.

[28] 2 Timothy 4:5 But you, keep your head in all situations, endure hardship, do the work of an evangelist, discharge all the duties of your ministry.

[29] James 5:16 Therefore confess your sins to each other and pray for each other so that you may be healed. The prayer of a righteous person is powerful and effective.

[30] John 11:33-35 When Jesus saw her weeping, and the Jews who had come along with her also weeping, he was deeply moved in spirit and troubled. Where have you laid him? he asked. Come and see, Lord, they replied. Jesus wept.

[31] Luke 19:41-42 As he approached Jerusalem and saw the city, he wept over it and said, If you, even you, had only known on this day what would bring you peace—but now it is hidden from your eyes.

[32] John 2:14-17 In the temple courts he found people selling cattle, sheep

and doves, and others sitting at tables exchanging money. So he made a whip out of cords, and drove all from the temple courts, both sheep and cattle; he scattered the coins of the money changers and overturned their tables. To those who sold doves he said, 'Get these out of here! Stop turning my Father's house into a market!' His disciples remembered that it is written: 'Zeal for your house will consume me.'

[33] Romans 12:15-16 Rejoice with those who rejoice; weep with those who weep. Live in harmony with one another. Do not be proud, but enjoy the company of the lowly. Do not be conceited...

[34] Genesis 11:3-4 They said to each other, 'Come, let's make bricks and bake them thoroughly.' They used brick instead of stone, and tar for mortar. Then they said, 'Come, let us build ourselves a city, with a tower that reaches to the heavens, so that we may make a name for ourselves.'

[35] Acts 6:3 Brothers and sisters, choose seven men from among you who are known to be full of the Spirit and wisdom. We will turn this responsibility over to them.

[36] Colon-Emeric, Edgardo. Speech. 2015 Duke Divinity School Baccalaureate Service. Presented at the 2015 Duke Divinity School Baccalaureate Service, May 11, 2019.

[37] Luke 5:15-17 Yet the news about him spread all the more, so that crowds of people came to hear him and to be healed of their sicknesses. But Jesus often withdrew to lonely places and prayed.

[38] Breen, Mike. Essay. In *Building a Discipling Culture: How to Release a Missional Movement by Discipling People like Jesus Did*, Kindle 1371–72. Greenville, SC: 3DM Publishing, 2017.

[39] A similar quote is attributed to John Maxwell.

[40] Ecclesiastes 4:12 Though one may be overpowered, two can defend themselves. A cord of three strands is not quickly broken.